# BEHIND THE SCREEN

# BEHIND THE SCREEN

## HOLLYWOOD INSIDERS ON FAITH, FILM, AND CULTURE

Edited by
SPENCER LEWERENZ and
BARBARA NICOLOSI

**BakerBooks**
Grand Rapids, Michigan

Published by Baker Books
a division of Baker Publishing Group
P.O. Box 6287, Grand Rapids, MI 49516-6287
www.bakerbooks.com

Printed in the United States of America

Library of Congress Cataloging-in-Publication Data
Behind the screen : hollywood insiders on faith, film, and culture / edited by Spencer Lewerenz and Barbara Nicolosi.
     p.   cm.
  Includes bibliographical references.
  ISBN 0-8010-6547-X (pbk.)
    1. Hollywood (Los Angeles, Calif.)—Religion. 2. Actors—United States—Religious life. 3. Motion pictures—Religious aspects—Christianity. 4. Film criticism. 5. Christianity and culture. I. Lewerenz, Spencer. II. Nicolosi, Barbara.
  BR560.H64B44 2005
  261.5′7—dc22                        2005018708

"The Hollywood Divide" by Ron Austin is a revised version of a speech given at the 2003 "Mere Entertainment" conference, sponsored by Act One and Fuller Theological Seminary and held at the Mears Center at Hollywood Presbyterian Church. It appeared originally in *Image Quarterly*.

# Contents

112811

Contents

# Introduction

So you thought the only Christians in Hollywood were Christian Slater and Christian Bale. Then this book caught your eye, with its claim of being written by Christians in the entertainment industry. And now you're wondering: who are these people, and what are they doing *there?*

Or maybe you picked up the book because you're aware of what's going on in Hollywood. You know that Christians helped make movies like *X-Men* and TV shows like *Joan of Arcadia* and *That '70s Show.* Maybe you even recognize some of the names in the table of contents.

But if you do, you're in the minority, because for the most part, Christians don't like Hollywood.

Here's the situation as many see it (and if you don't think this way, you probably know plenty of people who do):

- Most movies and TV shows are immoral, obscene, perverted, or some combination of the three (except *7th Heaven*).

- Hollywood has it out for Christians in much the same way Tom had it out for Jerry or Foghorn Leghorn had it out for the dog.
- The entertainment and news media are controlled by the "cultural elite," a cadre of ex–Ivy League dandies who, when not swiping manger scenes from suburban lawns, spend their time in idle cocktail chatter sneering at "conventional morality" and Costco.

We obsess about "the culture" endlessly; we analyze and criticize. But we can't figure out anything to do but point an accusatory finger at Hollywood. If this were a scene from an old-time movie serial, our culture would be tied to the train tracks, Hollywood would be twirling its moustache, and we'd be in the corner with a petition sign.

Blaming Hollywood for our cultural woes has become a habit. And, as Bob Briner observed in his 1991 book *Roaring Lambs*, it's a bad one. Casting Hollywood as the enemy has only pushed Hollywood farther away. And the farther Hollywood is from us, the less influence we have on our culture. We've left the business of defining human experience via the mass media to people with a secular worldview. Is it any surprise that when we turn on the TV, we see people act like they have a secular worldview?

Nor have we exactly endeared ourselves to Hollywood by blaming them. Ever notice how Christians in movies tend to fall into two categories: psychos and inbred psychos? If you've never had a Christian friend—or, for that matter, even met a Christian—and if all you know of them is angry, hateful protests, you might think that they're angry, hateful people.

How ironic that we, who were called to be examples of love for the world, have come to represent all that is cold and hateful in the popular imagination. And is there not some truth in it? In pushing away secular Hollywood, haven't we turned our backs on the very people Christ called us to minister to—the searching and the desperate, those without the gospel's saving grace and truth?

Blaming Hollywood has to be considered a failed tactic that needs to be abandoned.

In 1999, a small group of Christian writers and producers in Hollywood discovered that they shared a common conviction. If there is to be spiritual renewal within Hollywood, it must come from within Hollywood. The protests, letter campaigns, and finger-pointing don't do any good; change, they decided, can only start on studio lots, in network offices, at talent agencies, and on movie sets.

They rejected the notions floating in some Christian circles of "infiltrating" or "conquering" Hollywood. The people in the entertainment industry, they recognized, are just as important as the products coming out of it. Their purpose would be to transform Hollywood, not to take it over.

To do this, they would need people, and not just any people. People who would be both apostles and artists; people with a heart for the industry, who in their work would devote themselves to truth and beauty, while in their lives would strive to be examples of Christ's love and truth.

And so this small group of Christians started a nonprofit program called Act One to train these "artist-apostles" for Hollywood. Six years later, Act One had scores of alumni in various positions within the industry. Some were signed to major talent agencies, and others were writing major studio releases.

Written by Act One faculty, edited by Act One staff, and developed from the Act One curriculum, this book is the fruit of the prayer, discernment, and discussions that have come out of this new community.

It wasn't long after our first summer program that people began to say things like "You should really sell tapes of your classes" or "I can't leave the ostrich farm to come take your course—is it online?" We needed some way of sharing what we do with Christians everywhere.

So here it is. *Act One: The Book.* Or, as we prefer to call it, *Behind the Screen: Hollywood Insiders on Faith, Film, and Culture.*

The project began four years ago as a proposal for a Christian screenwriting manual. "The audience is too small. No one will publish that," we were told, as if we had pitched a book on "How to Frame Your Bea Arthur Belt Buckle Collection." So, we asked ourselves: what about Act One would be of interest to more than just Christian artists? That's when we first realized what this book could be.

Act One had already been engaging the broader church in a conversation about faith, entertainment, and culture. We'd been speaking and doing interviews all over the country, and each time the response was overwhelming. Everybody wanted to hear from the Hollywood Christians, because everybody has a stake in what goes on in Hollywood.

We realized people would be even more eager to hear from our faculty members, the TV writers, directors, screenwriters, producers, script consultants, who live in the thick of it. If we had each of them write something about Hollywood and Christians, we would have a book.

So, we approached them with the tentative title *What Hollywood Needs* and asked for possible essay topics. As the proposals streamed in, everybody seemed to be saying the same thing in a different way: what Hollywood needs shouldn't concern us as much as what the church needs.

Some suggested that Christians need a deeper understanding of different aspects of Hollywood. Others suggested we change the way we approach Hollywood in one way or another. And more than a few offered a combination of the two. Whatever the case, each essay revolved around the idea that if we are to transform Hollywood, we must first transform ourselves.

In a way, this brought us full circle, back to that question we asked ourselves six years ago: what can we do? What can Christians do about our culture? Some of us started a training program. The following essays will make some other suggestions.

Read on, think it over, and then it will be up to you to do something new.

Spencer Lewerenz and Barbara Nicolosi
Hollywood, California

# 1  Changing the Channels

## Dean Batali

Christians are always telling me that they don't watch TV. Some of them proudly boast that they have unplugged their television sets. A few even claim to have thrown their sets into the garbage.

You know what I think they should do?

Dig the thing out of the trash. Plug it back in. Watch more.

I will admit to a certain level of prejudice on this issue, since I've been making my living as a television writer for nearly ten years. If too many people stop watching, I'll be out of a job, and then what is my mother going to tell her friends?

But I would like television watchers—especially those who are Christians—to speak up more. Let Hollywood know what you want to see on TV. Let them know when you see something you don't like, and send them praise when they deserve it.

---

Dean Batali is executive producer of Fox's *That '70s Show*. He also wrote for the initial two seasons of *Buffy the Vampire Slayer* (WB).

As it is, the ones who have gotten rid of their TVs or simply do not watch because "there's nothing good on" are, essentially, just looking the other way. And you can ask the guy bleeding on the side of the road to Jericho how much good that does.

People ask me, "How come TV is so bad?" But not enough of them ask, "What can I do to make it better?"

Well, thanks for asking.

The first step is to understand that TV is just a delivery system for ads. The only programming that really matters to those in power is the commercials (except on pay cable channels like HBO, where nothing matters except how many people subscribe). The success of a show is not measured by how good it is, or who says they loved it, or even how many people watch. A show is a success if the people who watched it go and buy the products that were advertised during the commercials. It is all about what is being sold and (just as important) who is doing the buying.

This is why a show like *7th Heaven*—which was the highest-rated show on the WB network for years—was never considered as much of a success as *Buffy the Vampire Slayer* or *Dawson's Creek*, two lower-rated shows on the same network. The perception was that the audience for the latter two shows had more money to spend, so advertising rates were higher, and therefore the shows were more profitable. It might not seem fair, but viewers need to understand that the most-watched shows aren't always considered the most financially successful. Certain kinds of audiences are perceived as being more desirable—that is, have more money to spend—and certain kinds of audiences are hardly desirable at all.

Guess where Christians fit in.

A few years ago, I sat with my (now former) agent and told him I wanted to write shows about people who believe in God. His first response? "Well, that's going to be a tough sell." This was before *The Passion of the Christ* broke box office records. But remember, before that film made several wineskins full of money, it was considered a tough sell too.

That same year, *Will and Grace* was one of the highest-rated sitcoms on TV, and *Queer as Folk* and *Sex and the City* were two of the biggest things on cable. But shows about people who believe in God—that would appeal to the vast majority of Americans who believe in God—were going to be a "tough sell."

"Television is *broad*casting," my agent explained, as if I needed some sort of *Schoolhouse Rock* education. "They are trying to reach the greatest common denominator."

"There are one hundred million people in America who go to church every week," I said. "Isn't that 'broad' enough to 'cast' for?"

"Well," he said, "the thing is, Christians don't consume the way everybody else does."

I nearly dropped my Coke on my Nikes.

My agent explained that, in the eyes of advertisers, Christians are a homogeneous group hanging out somewhere in the South who don't watch TV. And even if they did watch TV, they still wouldn't spend that much money.

My agent had a point (though I didn't tell him at the time). Christians may spend just as much as everybody else on toothpaste and toilet paper, but we probably don't spend as much on beer and movies and luxury cars—and those are three industries that drive the advertising market. A case could be made that the average Christian household does not have as much disposable income as other households. Christian homes are more likely to be single-income—with one parent at home caring for the kids.

(Oh, and let's not let this secret out: Christians, if they are truly faithful, are going to be consuming 10 percent less than their neighbors down the street, because that's how much we should be giving to the church.)

This exchange with my agent (did I mention he's now my former agent?) made me realize that Christians need to let Hollywood know that we are just as "broad" as the next guy and that they should start "casting" to us.

How do we do this? First, Christian viewers need to discover that a few things on TV are quite good. You just have to look hard to find them. Consider this: broadcast TV (that is, the main networks—the channels you can get for free with an antenna or through basic cable) airs about ninety hours of programming a week. That doesn't even take into account the shows on cable TV. Now, a lot of these shows aren't very good. But most of the art and entertainment produced throughout history hasn't been very good. (If you were forced to listen to every song ever written or look at every painting ever painted, imagine how much garbage you'd have to sift through.) A few television programs, however, are quite good—consistently better than most movies, books, or plays. You just have to know where to look.

That means you have to read reviews—in newspapers and magazines or on the Internet—and actually watch the shows the critics say are good. Of course, the critics aren't always right, but they can often point you in the right direction. The sad reality is that many of the best-reviewed shows of the past few years never found an audience. "There's nothing good on TV," I often hear people say. "Really?" I want to respond. "Have you seen everything?"

I sympathize with viewers who are disgusted with the foul language and sexual content on many television shows. That's one of the reasons I came to Hollywood—to try to influence the content of TV shows. But viewers who never tuned into

*NYPD Blue* because of the controversy over its subject matter missed out on one of the most redemptive (and specifically Christian) story lines on TV. Think of the impact that could have been made if ABC and the producers of the show had received as many compliments for that story line as they did negative letters and threats of boycotts when the show first came on the air.

Another show, *Boomtown*, came and went with critical acclaim, having never found an audience. If Christians had been paying attention to certain episodes, they would have seen a main character praying and living out her Christian faith and another rediscovering his relationship with God and returning to church.

And there's nothing good on television?

As it is, Hollywood has assumed that Christians either aren't watching (because they rarely hear from Christians who have anything positive to say) or aren't offended enough by the bad stuff that is regularly on TV to do anything about it.

A network executive who knew my faith once asked me if I thought Christians would be offended by a certain joke in the script we were filming that week. "No," I mused, "but they might be offended by the pervasive drug use and rampant promiscuity on our show." He had stopped evaluating that aspect, because he was under the directive to give the audience what they want. And he admitted that, at least at this network, they assumed that the people tuning in knew what they were in for, and if they wanted other kinds of programming, they would be watching another channel.

In other words, to the people at that network, Christians didn't exist, and if they did, they were watching something else. (I'm not sure what they think we are watching, or why it doesn't occur to somebody to put something on the air that Christians might actually want to watch, but that discussion is for another fall season.)

The economic reality for the networks is that there are plenty of people who want to watch what they are airing, so why air anything else? There are millions of people who tune in to the networks every night, so the networks are just "giving the people what they want," right?

Not so fast. On any given week, the number-one show in America is watched by approximately thirty million people. That seems like a lot, but do the math. That means that more than two hundred million Americans are doing something else. Some were watching different shows; nearly half didn't even have the TV on.

Many of those who don't have the TV on are Christians. They probably have much better things to do with their lives, like complain about how bad television is. But if they sought out shows that reflected their values instead, Hollywood would have to take note. Somebody has to buy their toothpaste and toilet paper, and it might as well be us.

It's going to take time for things to change, mostly because the people in Hollywood have become so isolated from people of faith. I have worked with more than fifty-five writers in my career, and only three regularly attended church. Of those three, none would admit to being especially religious. Hollywood is a highly secular industry, and there is a huge disconnect between the people who make television and the people in the churches who might watch if only there were something better on.

As it is, TV programming reflects the worldview of the people writing it—and that worldview rarely includes God. (There are a few notable exceptions, like *Joan of Arcadia* and *Touched by an Angel*. But notice that those two prime-time network shows had to create supernatural fantasies in order for God to exist.)

I remember an episode of *ER* that began with four different couples in separate homes waking up in bed together. None of the couples were married, and one of the couples consisted of two lesbian women. The implication was that all of that behavior was morally acceptable, and I'm certain that's what the writer felt. His values trickle down into our culture, and simply turning off the TV doesn't stop the flow.

Essentially, writers write what they know. Too many of the writers I have met only know Christians as judgmental, narrow-minded, and hypocritical. The Christian characters we see on TV simply reflect that.

A writer I worked with once said to me, "I'm so glad I know you, because now I know that not all Christians are freaks." I just smiled and tried not to say anything that would make her change her mind.

(A few Christians have expressed similar sentiments after meeting me, since I put to rest their previous assumption that everybody who worked in Hollywood was a heathen freak. I tell them I'm not a heathen, but they should get to know me better before assuming I'm not a freak.)

I want to take this opportunity to encourage Christians to learn the craft of TV writing and come to Los Angeles to help make a difference. Or perhaps I should put it this way: PLEASE PLEASE PLEASE PLEASE PLEASE!

(I'm really lonely.)

But if becoming the next Rob Petrie isn't in the cards, there are some simple, specific things you can do if you want to see shows that reflect your values on TV. And the most effective thing you can do is actually refreshingly old-fashioned: write letters. Then, get them into the hands of the people who matter.

This will take some homework, but most of what you need to know can be found on the Internet or by calling information in Los Angeles. You can send letters directly to the writers of a show by mailing them to the production office of the show.

You can also send a letter care of the network, but it will take longer to get there—if it gets there at all. But you can pick any show, call the network on which it airs, and ask for the mailing address of the production office (or the phone number, so you can call the place yourself).

I have received only a few letters from viewers over the past ten years, but I have been in the room plenty of times when other writers have received them. We love it. And if the letter writer has a valid point of view presented in a polite way, it might make a difference in how we write in the future.

You should also write to the network that airs the show, and—to be most effective—address the letter to the president of the network (again, consult the Internet for this info, or call information in L.A.)

Here is how *not* to write a letter:

Dear Writer/Network President,

After watching last week's episode, I will never watch your sin-filled show/network again.
    Have you no soul, you pervert?

Love in Christ,
A Former Viewer

By admitting that you're never going to watch again, you are essentially letting the writer or executive know that you don't matter. Why should they change if you're not going to watch anyway?

Instead, begin your letter by praising the show. Tell them you are a fan of their work (or of other shows on the network). Then, express your disappointment in the subject matter or style of an episode. Let them know you want to remain a faithful viewer, but if there are many more episodes like the one that offended you, you may quit watching. If you express yourself in this manner, you will give the writers and the network incentive to do things differently.

And if you want to have an even bigger impact, send a copy of the letter to two or three of the advertisers on the show. Find the address of Coca-Cola or McDonald's or Procter & Gamble and address it to "Consumer Relations." You will almost certainly get a response, and you might even get a coupon for a free soda or a bar of soap.

Another faulty tactic is sending pre-written postcards or form letters. These are ignored—even if there is a campaign to send in hundreds or thousands. Save your stamps.

An episode of a show I worked on dealt with some graphic sexual behavior and carried a warning about "mature content." The network was concerned that there would be an outcry from viewers who found the show objectionable. They braced themselves for the onslaught of letters and calls. The show aired, and . . . nothing. Crickets. A rusty sign squeaking in front of an empty saloon as sagebrush blows across the desert.

Then, a little while later, they received a number of postcards from some organization protesting the content of our show. I'm not sure how many came in—a few dozen, at least—but I know the impact it had . . .

Cue those crickets again.

Organized protests mean almost nothing to the networks, but individuals who take the time to make a call or write and stamp a letter mean very much. If each of those people who had felt they were doing such good by sending a postcard had taken the extra few minutes to compose a short letter, and then the network started receiving letters from various corners of the nation—even if the total number was barely a dozen—it would have meant a lot.

Suppose you see something on TV that offends your sensibilities. You write a brief note and send it to the network and

21

the writer and/or the executive producer and an advertiser or two. And suppose you could find three or four friends or relatives around the nation who saw the same show and agreed with your point of view. Suddenly the network is hearing from California and Colorado and New Jersey and Tennessee, and somebody is going to start paying attention. And if the letter writers present themselves as Christians, the people at the networks might gradually realize that there are people who believe in God who live in California and New Jersey and not just Tennessee and Colorado.

And here's how to have an even bigger impact: do the same thing when you see something you like.

All this, of course, means you have to become an informed viewer. Watch a few minutes of a show here and there. Start talking with friends and family about what they have been watching. Certainly not all shows are worth watching. Some are harmful. And most of the time there are better things you could be doing than watching TV. But if you're concerned enough about the culture to have read this far, then you are probably looking for ways to change the culture. That means becoming informed.

I was having breakfast with an acquaintance from church who was complaining about the content of movies and dismissively waved a hand toward a nearby multiplex, saying, "I'm sure all of those movies have a sex scene in them." Actually, most of them did not, but he was too uninformed to know it. I suggested he subscribe to a weekly entertainment magazine, read reviews, and check out websites to learn more about what is out there before he complains. Otherwise, when the good stuff does come along, he's going to miss it.

Last time I checked, a lot of good stuff had come along. He missed it.

If we're not careful, Hollywood is going to assume there's no one out there who wants to see the good stuff. Let them know you're out there.

This is going to be a gradual journey. It seems absurd that Christians in America need to remind Hollywood that we exist, but that's the current state of things. Communicate with friends and relatives, seek out entertainment that elevates and edifies, and let the networks and studios know how much you love it. Then, the next time someone like me pitches a show to a network executive that is even more faith-affirming, that executive might remember the letter they got from Colorado, and the other one from New Jersey . . . And eventually they're going to end up selling a lot of toothpaste and toilet paper.

In the Dr. Seuss book *Horton Hears a Who*, the tiny world of Who-ville—no bigger than a speck of dust—is about to be boiled in a vat of scalding water by uninformed skeptics who don't believe Who-ville exists. All of the Whos join together and shout "We are here, we are here, we are here!" and are heard just in the nick of time, saving their world.

You think our culture is boiling over? Maybe we should all try shouting a little bit louder. But, you know, politely. And we probably don't really need to shout. Unless there's something really good on TV.

Imagine that.

# 2      Opportunity Lost

## Craig Detweiler

Nowhere has the rift between Hollywood and the Christian community been more visible than in the controversy surrounding Mel Gibson's *The Passion of the Christ*.

In January 2003, though Gibson was in the middle of filming, he took the time to appear on the conservative talk show *The O'Reilly Factor*. It seems that a reporter had been "digging through" his private life, even going so far as to approach his eighty-five-year-old father, looking for information that would make Gibson look like a bigot and discredit his film. O'Reilly

Craig Detweiler is associate professor and chair of mass communications at Biola University. He is also a screenwriter and the author of the book *A Matrix of Meanings: Finding God in Pop Culture*. He wrote the film *The Duke* for Buena Vista and *Extreme Days* for Providence Entertainment. His documentary *Williams Syndrome: A Highly Musical Species* won a Cine Golden Eagle and the Crystal Heart Award at the Heartland Film Festival. Craig serves as executive producer of the City of the Angels Film Festival and on the advisory boards for Reel Spirituality and the Heartland Film Festival. Craig has an MFA from the University of Southern California's School of Cinema/TV and an MDiv from Fuller Theological Seminary. He is a contributing editor for *The Mars Hill Review*. *A Matrix of Meanings*, co-written with Barry Taylor, was honored by the Evangelical Christian Publishers Association as one of five finalists for the 2004 Gold Medallion Book Award in theology/doctrine.

asked Gibson if the film would upset Jews, and he responded, "It may. But it's not meant to."

Gibson's appearance was all it took to convince the Jewish media that it was once more under attack by Christians who blamed them for the death of Jesus—and all it took to convince the Christian community that their beliefs were once more under attack by the liberal media. Overnight the media began speculating whether Gibson and his film were anti-Semitic, and overnight Gibson became the poster boy for Christians' frustrations with the media. By the time *New York Times Magazine* published the results of the reporter's "digging," Gibson had already begun screening the film for churches and conservative journalists. Based on their word of mouth, Christians officially adopted the film. The lines were drawn.

Rumblings from Hollywood indicated Gibson would have a hard time finding a distributor for the film. Fox, who usually handled Gibson's films, turned it down. Others reportedly wouldn't go near it. Christians' ire turned from the news media to Hollywood. Many recalled how Hollywood had rolled out the red carpet for *The Last Temptation of Christ*, a film they believed was blasphemous.

Gibson eventually struck a deal with Newmarket, a distributor of small indie films. Media speculation intensified. Many in Hollywood were saying Gibson would never work again. The cover of *Entertainment Weekly* asked, "Can Mel Gibson Survive *The Passion of the Christ*?" Meanwhile, the Christian community was making the movie an event, intent on sending Hollywood a message. Churches across the country bought out theaters in advance.

The film opened to megablockbuster numbers: $125 million in its first five days. It went on to make $610 million worldwide. Hollywood caved, picking up the film for DVD distribution. *Entertainment Weekly* proclaimed Gibson the most powerful person in Hollywood. The Christian community won.

Or did it?

*The Passion* was a brilliant movie, but for the Christian community, it was a missed opportunity. As followers of Christ, we should have used the controversy as a chance to better understand the Hollywood community and to build bridges with them. Instead, we used it as another tool in the culture war.

We cannot afford to miss another such opportunity. Christians must gain a better grasp of history, particularly Hollywood's prickly experience with American politics. We need to understand that Hollywood doesn't have a problem with Jesus; they have a problem with Jesus's people—or more accurately, with Jesus's people who subscribe to Republican politics. We need to understand that, for Hollywood's primarily Jewish community, every protest, boycott, or picket awakens ugly visions from the political past. When Christians talk boycott, Hollywood hears pogrom.

## The Beginning

The history of Hollywood begins in New Jersey, in Thomas Edison's "Black Maria" studio. In 1891, Edison applied for patents on a camera called the Kinetograph and a peephole viewer known as the Kinetoscope. Through the Kinetoscope, a single viewer could experience the illusion and joy of motion pictures. Unfortunately for Edison, he failed to see the potential for people to experience motion pictures as a group. It was France's Lumière brothers who introduced projection—and communal viewing—in 1895 with their Cinematographe. The big-screen experience we cherish as "cinema" was born.

So, why do we talk about Hollywood rather than Paris or West Orange, New Jersey? And how did an industry founded by a Victorian Christian like Edison end up dominated by Jewish immigrants? Edison may have owned the patents for motion picture production, but the film industry became a business dependent upon exhibition. Edison protected his control of film production with an aggressive legal strategy, but it would be in vain. He didn't own the theaters in which to play the films. Victorian Christians considered opera and the symphony legitimate art forms but cinema a novelty—a cheap, base amusement. Like vaudeville, such a questionable enterprise was seen as best left to immigrants. In the wake of European pogroms, young Jewish immigrants had flooded America's East Coast, drawn by the promises embodied by the Statue of Liberty. Yet, many newly arrived Jewish scholars, lawyers, and businessmen found themselves shut out of "legitimate" professions by none-too-subtle white/Anglo-Saxon/Protestant prejudice. Amusement arcades and vaudeville theaters provided viable entry-level jobs for hungry immigrants.

The rise of nickelodeons, nickel theaters dedicated solely to film exhibition, changed the burgeoning industry forever. By 1908, nickelodeons tallied eighty million admissions per week (when the entire U.S. population was one hundred million). Instead of buying films and running them until they scratched or broke, movie exhibitors needed a fresh, evolving supply of films that changed every week. Exhibitors would now rent rather than purchase films. The three-level production, distribution, and exhibition system was born (which remains in place today).

Edison made every effort to consolidate control of the industry. A combination of legal pressure, threats, and collusion allowed Edison to gather nine leading film companies (such as Biograph, Vitagraph, and Pathe) under one banner as the Motion Picture Patents Company. The Edison trust even formed an exclusive contract with George Eastman that guaranteed he would only sell perforated, raw film stock to the Patents Company. With production consolidated, Edison's Patents Company raised prices on distributors and exhibitors. The distributors and exhibitors rebelled against this monopoly. Jewish distributors and theater owners like Carl Laemmle and William Fox decided to become film producers, purchasing film stock from European suppliers. But how would they evade Edison's patents on cameras? The producers moved west, as far from Edison's East Coast power base as possible.

Southern California offered a variety of shooting locations, from the mountains to the sea. Los Angeles also offered plentiful sunshine (necessary because even interior shots were filmed outdoors, using the sun as the primary lighting source). Social conventions on the West Coast were fluid, driven more by money than birth, and Los Angeles was a perfect place for immigrants to reinvent themselves. Best of all, L.A. was a long way from the hired guns of the Edison trust.

Carl Laemmle formed the Independent Motion Picture Company (which morphed into Universal Studios), William Fox eventually merged with 20th Century, and Adolph Zukor formed Famous Players in Famous Plays, which later became Paramount. Neil Gabler traces the journeys of these movie pioneers in his seminal history *An Empire of Their Own: How the Jews Invented Hollywood*. Gabler chronicles the common background of the first movie moguls—their painful upbringing in Eastern Europe, the loss of their fathers, their flight from persecution, their desire to become mainstreamed Americans, and their massive financial success via the movies. By 1915, when the courts ruled that the Motion Picture Patents Company was an illegal trust, the independent Jewish producers were finally free of the Edison threat.

Recognizing film's tremendous potential as an evangelizing tool, Christian leaders urged churches to employ this new technology for evangelistic purposes. Writing in 1911, K. S. Hover claimed, "Satan has a new enemy. They are fighting the evil one with the flickering films that were formerly used only to amuse and in some instances to instruct. The moving picture machine has become a preacher and its sermons are most effective because they are addressed to the eye rather than the ear."[1] Finding movies an effective way to attract people to Sunday evening services, more and more churches purchased projectors.

D. W. Griffith's epics *Birth of a Nation* and *Intolerance* proved that this novelty was becoming an art form. Griffith introduced new techniques like close-ups and crosscutting, virtually creating a new visual language. Film's growing sophistication impressed Christians. A pastor writing in *Photoplay* (March 1920) dared to declare, "If Christ went to the 'movies,' He would approve." A Russian director Sergei Eisenstein adopted Griffith's editing techniques, creating dizzying montages in films like *Mother*, *Earth*, and *Battleship Potemkin*. But the Soviet propagandists' enthusiasm for the medium would last longer than that of American pastors.

With the introduction of synchronized sound in 1927, movies became more popular (and profitable) than ever. In the past, religious reformers had concentrated their efforts upon the evils of alcohol and evolution. With Prohibition overturned and the Scopes Trial a hollow victory over Darwinism, moral watchdogs turned their spotlight on Hollywood. Churches and theaters found themselves in competition for audiences, particularly on Sundays. Many religious leaders called for the rigorous enforcement of "blue laws" for keeping the Sabbath holy. Clergy encouraged their congregations to choose between the church and the theater.

The scandalous behavior of movie stars like Mary Pickford and Fatty Arbuckle only increased the anti-Hollywood sentiment. In 1920, Pickford's innocent "America's Sweetheart" image was damaged when she divorced her husband and married actor Douglas Fairbanks just three weeks later. Fatty Arbuckle went on trial for involuntary manslaughter after a wild San Francisco party that ended in the death of

Virginia Rappe. After three trials (the first two ending in a hung jury), Arbuckle was found not guilty. But he had already been convicted in the court of public opinion; his career as a comedian was over. By 1922, *The Sins of Hollywood* were chronicled in a best-selling book. In sermons and speeches around the country, Hollywood became "the devil's incubator," the source of moral degradation in America. In 1930, Catholic layman Martin Quigley and Daniel Lord, S.J., penned a series of moral guidelines for filmmakers known as the Hollywood Production Code. It governed depictions of sexuality and crime and recommended that the newly talking pictures stop using words like *God*, *hell*, and *damn*. Films were also expected to affirm religion and promote patriotism. In one tumultuous decade, Christians' relationship with Hollywood shifted from complimentary to competitive to contentious.

It's not hard to understand the studios' reaction to being policed by the church. Imagine it: having survived pogroms in Christian Europe, you come to America, the land of opportunity. You're handed the keys to the penny arcade, and those pennies soon add up. When Thomas Edison tries to tell you what you must show, you show Edison what you're capable of: you flee to California, land of the gold rush, defeat Edison in court, and become a millionaire one nickel at a time. And then, after all this, the church decides to make you the target of their latest crusade to clean up America. So you ignore their moral grandstanding—at least, as long as you can afford to.

Hollywood resisted the Code until it affected the bottom line. In 1933, the Catholic Legion of Decency threatened an economic boycott. With box office numbers already dropping due to the Great Depression, the Motion Picture Producers and Distributors of America (precursor of today's MPAA—the Motion Picture Association of America) hired the former postmaster general and national chairman of the Republican Party, Will Hays, to enforce the Code.

Hays's background as a teetotaling Presbyterian elder appeased Protestant protestors. In July 1934, the Hays Office hired Joseph Breen, a Roman Catholic newspaperman, as head of the new Production Code Administration. Note the troika of power involved: Jewish moguls hire a Roman Catholic to review their films and a Protestant to reassure the masses. The studios submitted their scripts and their finished films to Breen for a seal of approval. What resulted is now known as Hollywood's golden age, the classic studio era of *Stagecoach*, *Casablanca*, and *Gone with the Wind*.

The Production Code inspired the creation of new genres. Filmmakers forced to sublimate the sexuality in their scripts crafted the fast-paced comedies known as screwball comedies. Banished from falling into bed or even kissing for very long, characters instead fought with ingenuity and intensity. Sexual tension manifested itself in verbal battles and physical shtick. The films of Preston Sturges, George Cukor, and Howard Hawks continue to inspire today's romantic comedies, movies like *When Harry Met Sally* and *Sleepless in Seattle*.

Hollywood also altered America's self-perception through patriotic paeans toward the common man. Frank Capra's *Mr. Smith Goes to Washington* (1939) celebrated honesty, hard work, and the potential for one honest man to make a difference. Dramas like 1940s *The Grapes of Wrath* chronicled the journey of the Okies to California, declaring, "We're the people and we keep a-coming." Movie musicals like *Yankee Doodle Dandy* (1942) captured the patriotic fervor that accompanied World War II. Moviegoing exploded in popularity, becoming the national pastime. The movies defined America as a land of opportunity, champion of individuals and defender of the poor. Historian Neil Gabler relishes the irony. Jewish immigrants, shut out by the system and pressured by the church, present an idealized America that Catholics and Protestants embrace with such fervor that it eventually swallows up the real America. Movie mythology created by Jewish immigrants became the official version of U.S. history.

During World War II, Hollywood filmmakers served on the front lines of the propaganda war. Dramatic feature scripts were submitted to the Department of Defense for approval. Movies celebrated the efforts of the Allied forces, including France, Britain, and the Soviet Union. Americans united behind their GIs in movies like *Destination Tokyo* (1943), *Pride of the Marines* (1945), and *Objective Burma!* (1945). Movie stars joined the war effort, with Jimmy Stewart and Clark Gable earning medals for flying bombing missions over Germany. Directors Frank Capra, John Ford, and John Huston made classic documentaries like *The Battle of Midway* (1942) and *Prelude to War* (1943) reminding the United States "Why We Fight." As part of the effort, Hollywood adapted Russian documentaries for American audiences. The film *Moscow Strikes Back* (1942) even won an Oscar for Best Documentary.

After the war ended, the unity of the Allied forces proved short lived. Berlin was carved into pieces. Nazi scientists and their rocket technology were recruited by America and Russia. When the Soviets detonated an atom bomb in 1947, the Cold War ignited. Americans demanded to know who had given the Russians our bomb-making secrets. The House Un-American Activities Committee (HUAC), chaired by Republican congressman J. Parnell Thomas of New Jersey, conducted a thorough search in all levels of the government. Where else might Communists be hiding? Those pro-Russian films like *Moscow Strikes Back*, created with government support during the war, aroused suspicions. Hollywood was marked as a breeding ground for Communist spies.

The studio moguls, having survived pogroms, immigration, the Production Code, and World War II, were not about to sacrifice their financial freedom for the sake of politics. Republican execs Louis B. Mayer and Jack Warner agreed to testify before Congress and vowed not to employ any known or suspected Communists. Actors like Adolphe Menjou and Gary Cooper testified that they knew of communist activities amongst actors and writers. Ronald Reagan appeared as a friendly witness, cooperating with HUAC.

Nineteen filmmakers suspected of communist leanings were subpoenaed to Washington, D.C., as "unfriendly witnesses." Most were the sons of Jewish immigrants, familiar with the hard-fought freedom won by their parents. Most were also Communists, attracted to the artistry of Russian acting guru Stanislavski and supportive of the leftist guerrillas fighting in the Spanish Civil War. Eleven of those unfriendly witnesses subpoenaed were called to testify. Bertolt Brecht avoided the entire mess by fleeing to Germany. But ten other filmmakers appeared before Congress and pleaded for their right to remain silent, for the preservation of the secret ballot, and for the guarantees of the Constitution. They were held in contempt of Congress and sent to jail. For the Hollywood Ten, American politics became a bitter pill. Lauded as patriots while writing *Operation Burma!* and *Destination Tokyo* during the war, the Hollywood Ten found the political winds had shifted with a gale force. The land of freedom had robbed them of their livelihood, separated them from their families, and locked them in prison for exercising their guaranteed freedoms.

The conviction of the Hollywood Ten did not stop the witch hunt. The grandstanding efforts of Republican senator Joseph McCarthy of Wisconsin only heightened the tension. In an effort to cooperate with HUAC, Hollywood studios blacklisted hundreds of writers, directors, and actors, deeming them unemployable persona non grata. The acclaimed writers of patriotic films like *Mr. Smith Goes to Washington* and *The Grapes of Wrath* were now seen as the subversive authors of propaganda designed to undermine the government and rally the proletariat to rebellion. A few blacklisted writers kept working on the sly, often with the help of nonblacklisted writers who would be paid and credited for work created by a forbidden, blacklisted writer. Dalton Trumbo won an Oscar for writing *The Brave One* (1956) under the pseudonym Robert Rich. French author Pierre Boulle won the 1957 Oscar for Best Screenplay for *Bridge on the River Kwai*—even though he didn't speak English. The Writer's Guild of America has only recently restored the authentic, rightful credits.

## Not Forgotten

So why are there almost no Republicans in Hollywood? Surely the actions of Joe McCarthy and HUAC cannot continue to matter. Isn't that ancient history? An honorary Oscar awarded to director Elia Kazan in 1999 serves as a poignant test case. Kazan was perhaps the greatest director of actors in cinematic history. Born to Greek parents in Turkey, Kazan entered America at age four and graduated from Yale's prestigious drama school. He joined the Group Theatre, cofounded the Actors Studio, and directed seminal Broadway productions of *All My Sons*, *A Streetcar Named Desire*, and *Death of a Salesman*. His early films dealt with anti-Semitism (*Gentlemen's Agreement*), injustice (*Boomerang!*), and racism (*Pinky*). His left-leaning art (and politics) made Kazan an early target of the House Un-American Activities Committee. Kazan acknowledged and disavowed his former communist leanings, offering Congress a list of names of friends and colleagues he knew to be Communists. Kazan's testimony allowed him to continue working.

The ethical dilemmas surrounding Kazan's appearance before Congress find remarkable parallels in his classic film *On the Waterfront* (1954). Marlon Brando delivers a haunting performance as a washed-up boxer, Terry Malloy. Terry wrestles with his conscience, trying to decide whether to testify against his brother's organized crime syndicate. Brando's famous "I coulda been a contender" speech, delivered to his brother in the backseat of a car, remains one of the most captivating scenes in film history. *On the Waterfront* affirms the glory of the stool pigeon, turning Terry's (and Kazan's) testimony into the ultimate act of heroism. Hollywood awarded *On the Waterfront* eight Oscars, including honors for those who cooperated with HUAC, screenwriter Budd Schulberg and director Elia Kazan.

Forty-five years later, Kazan's honorary Oscar became a lightning rod for long-held grudges and unsettled issues to surface. Although given many opportunities to apologize to colleagues he had named, Kazan never fully recanted his actions. In a 1974 interview, Kazan demonstrated his equivocation:

> I had a choice between two evils—I've often since then, felt on a personal level that it's a shame that I named people, although they were all known, it's not as if I were turning them over to the police; everybody knew who they were, it was obvious and clear. It was a token act to me, and expressed what I thought at the time. Right or wrong, it wasn't anything I made up. I was convinced of it.[2]

As his honorary Oscar was being minted in 1999, costly full-page ads filled *Daily Variety* and *The Hollywood Reporter* asking Academy members to remember Kazan's betrayal. *The Village Voice* ran a cartoon of Kazan holding an Oscar and bearing a tail. The headline read "Hollywood's No. 1 Rat." On Awards night, when Kazan appeared onstage, the long, painful history of the blacklist reemerged. Avidly liberal stars like Robert De Niro and Warren Beatty stood in support of Kazan, the director who gave them their big break many years before. Yet, acclaimed actors like Nick Nolte and Ed Harris remained seated, scowling at the stage, still furious about Kazan's testimony. Steven Spielberg and Jim Carrey may have embodied the bulk of the audience's reaction, offering polite applause while never rising from their seats. For the greatest actor's director in the history of Hollywood, this amounted to the ultimate snub, payback for the 1950s. Kazan ended his short speech with the wistful reflection, "Maybe now I can just slip away."

The heated debates and painful histories swirling around the Shrine Auditorium on Oscar night were undoubtedly lost on most home viewers. Yet, Hollywood's justifiable obsession with the McCarthy era has found ample expression on the big screen. Films from the era like *High Noon* (1952) and *Invasion of the Body Snatchers* (1956) can be seen as thinly veiled commentaries on the HUAC hearings. Lone heroes, seen as crazy, try to wake up entire towns hoodwinked by fear, oblivious to the forces undermining society. *The Front* (1976), *Guilty by Suspicion* (1991), and *The Majestic* (2001) re-create the paranoia and pain of the proceedings, offering alternative readings of the 1950s. Why does Hollywood continue to tell the story of the blacklist? As Moses recounted the Exodus, contemporary Jews are simply retelling their story, so that no one will forget.

After writing fantasies like *Big* and *Dave*, Gary Ross made *Pleasantville* (1998), his directorial debut and his most personal statement. Many in the Christian community saw the film as an attack on family values, an attempt to undermine the nuclear family by celebrating sexual freedom and adultery. Christian film critic Phil Boatwright sensed, "Its producers are bent on convincing today's youth that the fifties were manned by lug heads who had no tolerance for personal freedoms."[3] Indeed. For Ross, the film was an opportunity to remember the legacy of his father, blacklisted screenwriter Arthur Ross. For those artists who've been literally imprisoned for their beliefs, *Pleasantville* stands as a defense of freedoms—of expression, of dissent, and of a color-blind society. Ross offers a harsh corrective to those who encourage America to turn back the clock, to return to the kinder, gentler ways of the 1950s. *Pleasantville* suggests that things were not so pleasant for people of color or for those who failed to conform to Christian standards. The 1950s may not be as innocent—or Christian—as people of faith recall. Ross believes, "Each era has its own false nostalgia. We all put a picket fence around something. For my generation it was the fifties, and for other generations it will be something else."[4] Certainly, those of us born after the fifties cannot imagine returning to a place and time we never visited except through reruns. Perhaps conservatives and Christians are calling America to return to a place that only existed in the movies, on television, in Hollywood's version of history. The odd irony returns.

The controversy over *The Passion of the Christ* presented the Christian community with an opportunity to build bridges with Hollywood's Jewish community. Yet Christians missed this opportunity due to their ignorance of Hollywood's painful history.

When *The Passion* stirred up Jewish fears of anti-Semitism, even before it arrived in theaters, Christians had a prime opportunity to see the relation between Jesus's suffering on the cross and the Jewish community's historic persecution. Yet, rather than acknowledge the sins of our fathers against the Hebrew people, the Christian community rallied around Mel Gibson and his persecution by the liberal press. We identified first and foremost with Mel's suffering at the hands of the Jewish intelligentsia. Still smarting from our own loss of cultural power, we put ourselves in Jesus's position, on the cross, at the very moment Jesus might have wanted us to claim our own culpability in the suffering of others. Jesus's call to corporate humility was twisted into a pep rally for those who wanted to win the culture war.

We embraced *The Passion of the Christ* as an unparalleled opportunity to transform a fallen culture. But we behaved like a persecuted minority committed to armed resistance. We claimed victory at the box office but lost out on the opportunity to bridge the gap between the Christian church and Jewish Hollywood.

When the Anti-Defamation League accuses *The Passion of the Christ* of inciting anti-Semitism sight unseen, they are attacking much more than a movie. They are attacking Mel Gibson and what his politics represent. When Mel Gibson defends his film on a conservative talk show like *The O'Reilly Factor*, he merely reinforces those fears of conservative intervention. Christians who justify the film's portrayal of the Jews as merely a reflection of the biblical record miss the oh-so-painful irony. Who killed Jesus? As *The Passion* ably demonstrates, the most sincere defenders of God joined forces with the ruling government to convict and crucify Jesus. The Pharisees and chief priests saw Jesus as a threat to God, a force that might undermine their religious tradition. Two thousand years later, conservative Christian groups team up with the government in order to preserve a traditional understanding of God and religion.

We wonder why Hollywood seems so defensive. Perhaps those who have been persecuted most thoroughly, most recently, are in the best position to identify the threats posed by God's most well-intentioned defenders. Many will continue a campaign to clean up Hollywood. While sorting out the splinters of sex, violence, and profanity, they are advised to remove a few massive historical logs along the way.

As a screenwriter who attempts to follow Jesus, I suggest that our apologetics should begin with apologies. *The Passion* portrays a Jesus who humbly embraces the cross. I hope and pray that the church can adopt a position of humility vis-à-vis Hollywood. St. Paul outlined an effective strategy for cultural engagement in his little-discussed, rarely memorized verse from 1 Corinthians 5:12: "What business is it of mine to judge those outside the church? Are you not to judge those inside?" The only sins we are responsible for are our own. After a hundred years of throwing stones at the culture, perhaps we can start a new century by owning our own complicity, confessing our own sins.

*The Passion of the Christ* concludes with a profoundly simple, poetic shot. A stone rolls away from the entrance to a tomb. A wind or spirit rises from underneath a burial wrap. The crucified Christ emerges healthy, whole, restored. This powerful, cinematic resurrection does not require any fireworks, pyrotechnics, or special effects. It is a quiet, private moment devoid of any grandstanding, protests, or politics. If the church adopts a quiet, humble attitude of confession and contrition, then perhaps a resurrection is possible—even in Hollywood.

### Notes

1. K. S. Hover, *The Silents of God: Selected Issues and Documents in Silent American Film and Religion, 1908–1925*, Terry Lindall (Lanham, MO: Scarecrow Press, 2001).

2. Elia Kazan, *Elia Kazan: Interviews*, ed. William Baer (Jackson, MI: University Press of Mississippi, 2000).

3. Phil Boatright, review of *Pleasantville*, *The Movie Reporter*, copyright 1998–2003 by CC Publications, www.moviereporter.com

4. Joshua Klein, "Inside *Pleasantville*," *The Onion A.V. Club*, October 21, 1998.

# 3    The Hollywood Divide

## Ron Austin

There has always been a Christian presence in Hollywood. In the so-called golden age, the thirties and forties, a Christian sensibility was clearly evident in the films of John Ford, Alfred Hitchcock, and Frank Capra—to name only the most prominent examples. There were also stars whose professional personae reflected spiritual values, such as Irene Dunne and Loretta Young. I once had the pleasure of introducing my late friend, Father Ellwood "Bud" Kieser, to an audience as "the best known Catholic priest in Hollywood since Bing Crosby." Bud liked that. Crosby and others such as Pat O'Brien had that kind of positive image.

Ron Austin is a veteran writer and producer with over a hundred credits in film and television. His television credits include the original productions of *Mission: Impossible*, *Charlie's Angels*, *Matlock*, and the *Father Dowling Mysteries*. He has more recently produced a documentary, *The Hidden Gift: War and Faith in Sudan*, and an experimental feature film, *Blue in Green*. A member of the Academy of Motion Picture Arts and Sciences, the Writers Guild, and the Directors Guild, he has been on the faculty of the USC cinema school and the American Film Institute. He has taught in the Act One program since its inception.

Later, the countercultural generation of the late sixties and seventies evinced suspicion of all institutions, especially of organized (that is to say, traditional) religion. The dissatisfied and rebellious baby boomers eventually became, and to some extent remain, dominant in Hollywood. Though now they *are* the establishment, they retain much of their anti-authoritarian posture.

To speak, as many do, of an antagonism between Christianity and an isolated Hollywood establishment is misleading. As I see it, the rift that emerged in those years reveals tensions between Christianity and much of popular culture itself. Hollywood has unquestionably played a role, but the roots of the conflict go deeper.

While Hollywood's subculture has become more open to spiritual values during the last decade, it bears a residual suspicion of religion in general and of Christianity in particular. Many Christians working or trying to work in the entertainment industry encounter some degree of prejudice. Based on personal experience of over a half century in Hollywood, I have theories about the sources of this conflict. Since I'm not a historian or a sociologist, I must employ the skills I've acquired during my years in what we locals call, with revealing provinciality, "the industry."

I'm going to frame this problem by recasting it as a dramatic conflict between two characters, a Christian and a Hollywood skeptic. Reverting to my previous roles, I'll treat the conflict as if I were a screenwriting teacher or a producer helping a writer to develop a script.

At the outset, we must recognize a built-in tension not unrelated to the story itself. Since the age of classical Greek theater, there have been two tendencies in drama: the Platonic and the Aristotelian. (I call them tendencies because these are not strict categories.) The Platonic tendency, which is attractive to many religious people, prefers drama to be a kind of model for behavior or guide to morals. As such, Platonic drama tends to be more ideal than real. Good is represented by the protagonist, and evil, or something akin to evil, by the antagonist. This useful, time-honored approach has produced some of Hollywood's best films. Ford and Capra, for example, often presented idealized heroes who struggled against corrupt villains. The Western genre is rooted in such mythic characterizations.

The other tendency, dominant in modern drama since Ibsen, Shaw, and Chekhov, has a different goal. It may offer some moral instruction, but its primary aim is to achieve what Aristotle called catharsis, a purgation of emotions. This more subjective process leads us into our own inner conflicts. Such a drama allows us, through the relative safety of art, to explore our own fears and desires. Through our identification with the characters, this process purges our hidden, primal feelings, or at least brings them forth so that we might confront them. At its best, this purgation leads to insight, but it does not necessarily offer a clear moral message.

Christians have tended to be more comfortable with Platonic dramas. You often hear religious commentators criticize what seem to them to be excesses of the Aristotelian tendency: "Why do you want us to see such ugly things?" they ask. Or, "Why do you have to use such bad language?" They are asking, not unreasonably, for a story that presents a model of good behavior, particularly for a young audience. What they don't understand is that Aristotelian drama needs to confront us with the ugly and unpleasant if it is to take us to those dark places requiring purgation.

As we can see, the two tendencies are often in conflict.

In the story I'm sketching now—of the rise of antipathy between the Christian and the secularist in Hollywood—the approach I propose is Aristotelian. I'm not going to offer a tale in which the Christian embodies virtue and the secularist corruption. I want real characters who will provoke us to explore our own inner lives. If we were to develop our story fully, these characters might each make good decisions and bad ones, behave honorably and deplorably. But we won't get that far, at least not here. In the initial stage of character development, our task is to allow the characters to grow, and so we must proceed without too much prior judgment. We don't know where these characters are going to lead us.

As a producer or teacher, I try to guide scriptwriters toward the deepest levels of conflict in their stories, which means probing the unresolved tensions within each character. Writers know this process to be long, difficult, and painful, and I'll abbreviate it here. In developing a character, a writer must first ask what the character wants, which usually has to do with what the writer wants. Much here depends on the writer's capacity for self-awareness. The process should eventually reach the point where the writer courageously addresses the deepest fears of the characters, which are closely related to his or her own concerns.

In a well-written script that deals with two characters in conflict, the story will not simply be about the clash between the goals and desires of the characters, but it will instead be a more profound confrontation. A mature scriptwriter will look more deeply, working to figure out what each character finds in the other that is somehow missing in himself, what weakness or uncertainty. Usually it's an unresolved inner conflict that, when triggered, is then projected onto the adversary. I call this mirroring.

Mirroring forms the basis of many classic genres. Take romantic comedy, for example (not farce, mind you, but comedy involving real character conflict). Our hero, though attracted to the heroine, finds himself troubled when faced with feminine traits like tenderness and sensitivity that are missing, or at least repressed, in himself. The man, confounded by having to grapple with this mirror of his missing traits, asks himself in ultimate frustration, "What does she want?" Or sometimes, "What do women want?" That he never fully grasps this provides the basis for comedy. Conversely, the woman, also sensing something missing, usually asks at some point, "Why doesn't he understand how I feel?" Because the man in a romantic comedy seldom does. These gender conflicts may be stereotypical, but they illustrate the process by which each character projects his or her inner conflict onto the other. This mirrored "battle of the sexes" has had audiences laughing since Aristophanes's day, if not before.

I want to use the idea of mirroring to explore our two characters, the Christian and the Hollywood secularist. By a secularist, I mean someone who has not grown up in a religious tradition or (as is quite common in Hollywood) has rejected religion. I do not mean someone of another religious faith. In present-day Hollywood, the secularist is unlikely to hold an opposing ideology or even a fully coherent philosophy. Rather than creating a debate, I want to understand the source of the hostility between these characters. To do so, I must first explore the inner conflicts of each, which the characters project onto each other.

The Christian (I suspect from personal experience) will have at least two largely unresolved conflicts. From a historical point of view, these conflicts come out of the confrontation between Christianity and the Enlightenment that produced modern culture. Hollywood, in many ways, is the embodiment of the best and worst of modernity, both its freedom and its irresponsibility. I seldom defend Hollywood, but I will do so here on the basis of two of its ideals, personal freedom and inclusion, which I consider the gifts of modernity. These two principles, valued to the point of being absolute by the secularist, produce inescapable inner conflicts for the Christian. This is ironic since, however misapplied, these two ideals arise from the Christian gospel.

The concept of personal freedom is largely derived from the Judeo-Christian ideas of free will and the God-given dignity of the individual. For Christians, the incarnation gives us our ultimate dignity, revealing the human as created in the image of God. Nonetheless, freedom presents us with a conflict. Our idea of freedom and its legitimate use differs from the secularist's. For the Christian, freedom is not an absolute good in itself. Rather, freedom of intellect and conscience is a means of coming to the truth, a truth embodied by Jesus and expounded in the Gospels. As Christians, once we encounter that truth, we see that it has requirements, even commandments. It makes demands on us that may in fact limit the use of our freedom. We don't have the liberty to create our own world. We discover truth; we don't invent it. And once we discover it, we are bound by the limits it reveals.

This produces conflict, inwardly and in society. I'm not speaking abstractly; I often see this conflict acted out by aspiring Christian writers. Many feel restricted and inhibited, even afraid of their own freedom. They fear that freedom will lead them to areas that they would rather not explore, or possibly even to condemnation by their church. This anxiety prevents them from exploring those places that involve risk. As a result, there is, in our Christian character, a button to be pushed. We have a fear of misusing our freedom, and perhaps a deeper fear of exploring the dark places in ourselves. We know that we can use our faith as a defense against the harsher aspects of reality to which we feel vulnerable. All this plays into the secularist's stereotype of believers as repressed, provincial, and inhibited people, afraid to confront the whole of life and hiding inside the church. As unfair as this caricature is, it hits a sore spot, touching on our inner fear and producing defensiveness and antagonism.

The Christian's other unresolved inner conflict relates to the question of inclusion. In the West, the ideal of inclusion has been enshrined as an absolute good nearly as reverently as freedom. At the contemporary table, everyone is invited, and any hint of elitism or segregation is anathema. Society is hardly consistent in achieving this goal, but the effort is persistent. Again ironically, the compassionate inclusion of outsiders, of strangers and sinners, has its foundation in the Scriptures and is at the heart of Christianity.

But this passionate secularist stance brings another Christian inner conflict to the surface. In the first place, we're not moral relativists. To us, inclusion doesn't mean condoning every behavior. For that matter, we don't even believe that all religions or moral views are equal. We are capable of great respect for other faith traditions, but we don't weigh them as equal with the truth we receive from Christ. This is the hard truth of the matter, and we have to face it. Our necessary stubbornness on this question puts a high wall between secularists and ourselves.

We ask ourselves regretfully whether we must always be walled off from others. Or worse, we wonder if we are using our religious identity to keep a wall between ourselves and others. We're not always sure, and at times we have to make difficult decisions. And again we find ourselves vulnerable to stereotype, this time the stereotype of the small-minded, judgmental Christian. We may protest that this stereotype is unfair, but there is some truth in it. We Christians are, in too many ways, a divided people. We are also inclined to divide others into categories: good and bad, saved and damned. Within my own denomination, I often hear the question, "Well, what *kind* of a Catholic is he?" To be accepted, you need to perform a kind of ideological lodge handshake.

We have to be truthful. From the secular point of view, we are often a spectacle of division. This perception makes many of us uneasy, and it should, because we are called to be healers more than judges. We fear, however, that there is some truth in this perception, and again it makes us defensive. The walls that we would like to tear down become higher.

Now that I have sketched the Christian character, let me turn to the Hollywood skeptic. Our secularist has his personal reasons for being critical of Christianity, still the most influential and hence intrusive religion in our society. But what are his unresolved conflicts? I'm going to explore just two.

To understand the first requires some historical perspective. When I was a young man in Hollywood some fifty years ago, religion in general and Christianity in particular weren't so much denigrated as ignored. They were considered intellectually obsolete. I was a devout nonbeliever then and didn't convert until my middle years. I was very much an adherent of the "progressive" culture of Hollywood in the forties, a time when strong ideological convictions about the direction of history were prevalent. There were, in other words, powerful rivals of Christianity that offered hope and even claimed some prophetic insight as to the future of humanity.

Left-wing politics were popular in Hollywood, including some undigested Marxism and other more benign forms of utopianism. The engine of history was to be driven by science and technology, and a perfected world was just around the corner. It may seem strange to the younger generation that such transparently naive beliefs were once so prevalent, but they were. They're not prevalent anymore. Nor does the promise of sexual liberation hold its previous appeal. In the 1940s, wealthy and successful people in Hollywood might go to their psychoanalysts almost daily, convinced that the Freudian liberation of the ego from the id would solve their problems. Later, in the sixties, a conviction prevailed that if we could just rid ourselves of sexual inhibitions, a new utopia would emerge.

Today, these rival pseudo-religions have failed, and Hollywood is at the center of the crisis of modernity. That is to say, a crisis of disbelief. This is not simply a turning away from traditional religion. That happened a generation ago. The modern crisis comes from the loss of belief in the alternatives to religious faith. There is a lot of noise in Hollywood about politics, particularly of the ultra-liberal variety, but what I hear in that noise is the clamor of those who would drown out their despair. With a handful of idealist exceptions, few in Hollywood believe any longer that politics can answer the frailties of the human condition. The less the belief, the more the noise.

And this is the secularist's first unresolved conflict. It is revealed whenever he confronts anyone with a strong belief system. Any person who has a passionate faith that endows him or her with confidence or hope in the future will push this button. This secular character is needled by an ongoing crisis of disbelief in the same way that the Christian is needled by an unresolved ambivalence toward personal freedom. The secularist's problem is what to do with the freedom that he's made an absolute good. Does freedom point to anything beyond itself? Does it mean anything? Does it lead anywhere? Simply to encounter a person who has a confident and coherent belief in a reality beyond the individual triggers a great deal of anxiety and antagonism in the modern skeptic.

The other emotional trigger for the secular character goes to his most crucial conflict: the cross. The belief that suffering has meaning, whether or not we comprehend it, is for the nonbeliever the most objectionable of Christian tenets. Chateaubriand said that the genius of Christianity was in its use and transformation of suffering. The path of Jesus requires faith that there is redemption in suffering. It is the path we must take if we are to follow Jesus through Good Friday to the Easter resurrection. Suffering is at the heart of our Christian identity. For the secularist, deprived of the structure of belief, suffering is only something to be avoided at all costs.

At times, however, the secularist fears that all this running from suffering may be futile or, worse, may be running from a path of salvation. If only he could stop running and turn around. Even a momentary consideration of this possibility can produce great anxiety and confusion. It's terrible to fear that the thing you've spent your life running from, once confronted, would have been the answer to all your life's questions. This unresolved fear produces antagonism toward the Christian, and in reaction the secularist paints the Christian as a masochist, even a sadist, clearly no fun at all.

In an Aristotelian work, these mutual provocations, arising from the unreconciled conflicts within two characters, point us toward a possible story. I would hope that this particular story might reach a level where the conflicts could be better understood and might even induce compassion. I'm not sure where our story is going to go, but maybe this character analysis suggests an ending or the beginning of an ending.

If this script is to have any significance, it needs to move toward reconciliation. One of the characters must move the story forward by taking the initiative and reaching out to the other, and I think it must be the Christian. The secularist, even with the best of intentions, lacks a strong motivation to do so. The confident humanist of the past, simply out of good will, might have made a move toward reconciliation. He might have felt that the Christian could be liberated by the historical forces in which the humanist had such strong faith. But given today's prevailing skepticism, there's little in the present-day secularist's outlook to motivate him to act beyond self-interest or self-defense. It will be up to the Christian to risk lowering his defenses, admitting his uncertainties, and opening himself to the secularist's mirrored fears. He must do this without an agenda, without preaching, and without trying to win. If he can truly make himself one with his secular adversary, he will necessarily begin to face his own inner struggles.

Some interesting drama might result. Roles might be reversed, and both characters might be illuminated. The best realized ending would be when the Christian begins to see Jesus in the other, the Jesus in both of them—the same Jesus who is suffering within each of us. This ending might provide real hope for both characters.

For many of you reading this essay, the character I've been calling the Christian is yourself. And if this story has worked, it will provoke some questions for you—and for me as well. For one, are we free and courageous enough to open ourselves to the suffering of our nonbelieving adversary? Doing so requires confronting our own unresolved inner conflicts, and perhaps much more.

I think the creative process requires that we do this if we are to write honest scripts and make good films. But, whether or not we're making films, this is what Jesus and the Gospels ask of us.

# 4 Why Do Heathens Make the Best Christian Films?

## Thom Parham

*Places in the Heart* is a film about Edna Spalding (Sally Field), a young woman who tries to save her farm from foreclosure after her husband dies. During the course of the film, Edna assembles a surrogate family around her, consisting of Moze, a black sharecropper (Danny Glover); Mr. Will, a blind boarder (John Malkovich); and her precocious children, Frank and Possum (Yankon Hatten and Gennie James). Near the end of the movie, the Ku Klux Klan runs Moze out of town. In the final scene, the townspeople gather at church, where a stirring rendition of "Blessed Assurance" is followed by a reading of 1 Corinthians 13:1–8:

Dr. Thom Parham is an associate professor of Theater, Film and Television at Azusa Pacific University. He has written for the CBS drama *JAG* and the Family Channel sitcom *Big Brother Jake* and has also worked on *Touched by an Angel*. Thom is listed in the 2002, 2004, and 2005 editions of *Who's Who Among America's Teachers*.

Though I speak with the tongues of men and of angels and have not love, I am become as a sounding brass or a tinkling cymbal. And though I have the gift of prophecy and all knowledge but have not love, I am nothing. And though I bestow all my goods to feed the poor and have not love, it profit me nothing. Love is patient, kind. Love is not jealous or boastful. Love never ends.

The choir then sings "I Come to the Garden Alone" as the communion elements are passed. Philandering husband (Ed Harris) is the first to partake, followed by his forgiving wife (Lindsay Crouse) and their daughter. The camera pans across various congregants, including an evil banker (Lane Smith) who tried to foreclose on Edna's farm, and band members from a previous night's shindig. Then, oddly, the camera continues to pan, revealing a couple who died trying to escape from a tornado, some of the Klansmen, and Moze. Panning past Mr. Will, Possum, Frank, and Edna, the camera finally rests on Edna's late husband, Royce (Ray Baker), and Wylie (DeVoreaux White), the black youth who accidentally shot him and was in turn lynched.

At this point, we realize there's much more going on in *Places in the Heart* than what's on the surface. The film is a metaphor for the kingdom of God, and the final scene tells us that God's grace is available to all who accept it—white or black, young or old, good or evil, living or dead.

Writer/director Robert Benton is not an evangelical Christian. Yet, his film incorporates "Christian themes" with more subtlety, artistry, and depth than the majority of films being made by professed Christians. It is not the only one. In fact, most films that successfully incorporate religious themes are made by nonreligious people.

Here are some of the better films with Christian messages or themes from the past few decades:

*Chariots of Fire* (1981)
*Tender Mercies* (1983)
*Places in the Heart* (1984)
*Hoosiers* (1986)
*The Mission* (1986)
*Grand Canyon* (1992)
*The Shawshank Redemption* (1994)
*Dead Man Walking* (1996)
*The Apostle* (1998)
*The Prince of Egypt* (1998)
*The Iron Giant* (1999)
*Magnolia* (2000)
*Signs* (2002)
*Jonah: A Veggie Tales Movie* (2002)
*About Schmidt* (2002)
*Changing Lanes* (2002)
*In America* (2002)
*Bruce Almighty* (2003)
*The Lord of the Rings* trilogy (2001–2003)
*The Passion of the Christ* (2004)

All of these films were critically acclaimed and/or box office hits. But with the exception of *Jonah*, *Bruce Almighty*, and *The Passion*, none were made by Christian filmmakers. Christians, however, did make these films:

*Gospa* (1995)
*Entertaining Angels* (1996)
*The Omega Code* (1999)
*The Joyriders* (1999)
*Left Behind: The Movie* (2000)
*Carman: The Champion* (2001)

*Megiddo: The Omega Code 2* (2001)
*Mercy Streets* (2001)
*To End All Wars* (2001)
*Hometown Legend* (2002)
*Joshua* (2002)
*Left Behind II: Tribulation Force* (2002)
*Luther* (2003)
*Finding Home* (2003)
*Therese* (2004)

Overall, these films are unwatchable. There are only a handful of good scenes among them. None had success with critics or at the box office. (What does it say about Christian filmmakers that one of their best-received movies features computer-generated vegetables who sing and dance?)

If Christians want to make successful films that incorporate their worldview, why not learn from those who are already doing it—non-Christians. So let's ask: why are the best Christian films being made by secular filmmakers?

The first reason secular filmmakers are making better Christian films is because they are making them for mainstream audiences.

All of the films on my first list were produced for the mainstream market. They opened in either wide theatrical release (over two thousand theaters) or, in the case of the smaller films, an "art house" release of around one thousand theaters. The films on my second list were produced for the "Christian market." A few were released into about three to four hundred theaters. Most went straight to video or got a "vanity" release in two or three theaters.

The idea that Christians will go see films targeted at them has not been borne out by the marketplace. Christians, it turns out, see the same films as everyone else.

And what about the success of the Christian music and publishing industries? They have succeeded because they take advantage of an infrastructure of Christian bookstores, through which music and books targeted at Christian audiences can be sold. But there are no Christian movie theaters, and Providence Entertainment, the lone Christian distribution company, recently imploded. In other words, films targeting Christians have to compete with mainstream films for distribution and, if they make it to the cineplex, for audiences.

But Christian filmmakers seem to believe that they do not have to compete in the mainstream market. Thus, storytelling and production values end up taking a backseat to the movie's message. The films are merely bait to lure viewers to a homily or altar call, and this only ensures their failure.

Even with the built-in distributions system of Christian bookstores, the Christian music and publishing industries figured out after a few years that they had to develop products that were just as good as mainstream books and music in order to succeed. Christian filmmakers will have to do this and more. To compete in the mainstream market, they will have to appeal not only to Christians but also to mainstream audiences.

## Parables, Not Propaganda

"If you want to send a message, try Western Union," said Frank Capra, a Christian who made hugely popular mainstream films. Film excels at metaphor—forging a connection between dissimilar objects or themes. It doesn't fare as well with text messaging. Show, don't tell, is the rule of cinema. Christians, however, can't seem to resist the prospect of using film as a high-tech flannel board. The result is more akin to propaganda than art, and propaganda has a nasty habit of hardening hearts.

Though *Places in the Heart* is a metaphor for the kingdom of heaven, nowhere is this notion communicated overtly. It is suggested through the film's system of metaphors and reinforced by its enigmatic ending. This is yet another reason non-Christians make the best Christian films: they understand that cinema is an art form of symbol and metaphor.

Jesus began many of his parables with the phrase, "The kingdom of God is like ..." (He used this construct twelve times in the Gospel of Matthew alone.) In the book *All the Parables of the Bible*, Herbert Lockyer explains, "Because of His infinity, God had to condescend to those things with which man was familiar in order to convey the sublime revelation of His will."[1] Jesus's parables allowed his audience to understand heavenly principles in earthly terms. He would even respond to questions with parables—instead of stating the answer outright, he would allow his audience to make the connections themselves. Jesus also knew that the things of heaven are too large to be fully grasped by the human mind. They are mysteries, in the classic sense of the word, and can only be hinted at through symbols and metaphors.

Christian filmmakers seem to dislike mystery. Rather than using Jesus's construct, "The kingdom of God is like ...," their films often proclaim, "The kingdom of God *is*." Nothing is left to the imagination. Audiences are not allowed to make their own connections; they are told what to think. In his book *True Believers Don't Ask Why*, John Fischer characterizes this attitude as: "Jesus is the answer; therefore nothing can be left unanswered." This approach, no matter how sincere, rings false to audiences and leaves them feeling manipulated. That's why movies like *Left Behind*, which try to convince audiences of the truth, instead leave them tittering. Anthony Breznican of the Associated Press described it as "a weak proselytizing device masquerading as a movie."[2] The *National Review*'s Rod Dreher called it the "Gospel According to Ned Flanders."[3]

As long as people of faith are more concerned with messages than metaphors, they are doomed to make bad films.

## "Do You Have Eyes but Fail to See?"

Secular filmmakers tend to observe life more objectively than Christians. They see the world the way it really is, warts and all. Christian filmmakers, on the other hand, tend to see the world the way they want it to be. Ignoring life's complexities, they paint a simplistic, unrealistic portrait of the world.

The film *Joshua*, adapted by Christian filmmakers from a popular Christian book, poses the question, "What if Jesus's incarnation occurred in modern times?" Unfortunately the filmmakers' answer seems to be "Jesus came to make nice people nicer" (to quote my friend and colleague Craig Detweiler). Christian artists seem more interested in propagating warm fuzzies than dealing with tough questions. (If King David were alive in twenty-first-century America, would his psalms make it past the gatekeepers of the Christian music industry?)

Perhaps the problem can be attributed to the fact that many evangelicals believe it's a sin to question God. But this notion is not scriptural. Jacob's name was changed to Israel—one who struggles with God—after his all-night wrestling match with the angel at Peniel. We are allowed to wrestle with God. Yet where are our stories about people of faith who struggle with God?

*The Apostle*, starring, written, directed, and executive produced by Academy Award winner Robert Duvall, is such a story. Although clearly familiar with evangelical subculture, Duvall is not a Christian. In the film, he plays Sonny, a pastor who discovers his wife has taken up with a youth pastor and conspired to take away his church. Sonny yells at God:

I'm gonna yell at you 'cause I'm mad at you. I can't take it.
Give me a sign or something. Blow this pain out of me. Give
it to me tonight, Lord God Jehovah. If you won't give me
back my wife, give me peace! Give it to me, give it to me,
give it to me, give me peace! Give me peace! I don't know
who's been fooling with me—you or the devil. I don't know.
And I won't even bring the human into this, he's just a mutt,
so I'm not even gonna bring him into it. But I'm confused,
I'm mad. I love you Lord, I love you, but I'm mad at you. I
am mad at you![4]

Sonny's dialogue evokes the book of Job. But today, the
candor and passion of his frustration with God could have
only been captured by a non-Christian. A Christian filmmaker
wouldn't dare create a Christian protagonist who questions
God, who falls or fails. But Duvall portrays a fully realized
character rather than a stereotype. Sonny accidentally kills
his wife's lover in a fit of rage. Yet, after Sonny flees from
prosecution, he continues to do the Lord's work.

Christians must not be afraid to grapple with the nature
of reality and, indeed, God himself in their art.

## The Wonders of God

Secular filmmakers also have an advantage when it comes
to making films based on Bible stories.

Sometimes it's difficult for those of us who grew up in the
church to truly appreciate the wonders, ironies, and paradoxes
inherent in our faith. God is the Creator of the heavens and
the earth. Christ was both man and God. These are not small
claims! But for those of us who believe them, they become so
second nature that they sometimes seem like it.

As a preacher's kid, I learned at an early age how to memo-
rize Scripture and find Bible verses. I came to think of the

parting of the Red Sea and the miracle of loaves and fishes as if they were everyday occurrences. It wasn't until I was older that I began to notice how amazing these biblical accounts sound to those who didn't grow up in a Christian household.

You can see this kind of wonder in *The Prince of Egypt*, an animated film from DreamWorks, a company owned by three secular Jews: Steven Spielberg, David Geffen, and Jeffrey Katzenberg. In one scene, we see the burning bush reflected in Moses's eyes as he realizes for the first time that this is YHWH, the Great I Am, the God of Abraham, Isaac, and Jacob. The sequence is everything it should be: ethereal, beautiful, and mysterious. Christian filmmakers will have to learn to see with new eyes if they want to convey the same sense of wonder in their biblically based films.

### The Need for Redemption

In our postmodern, relativistic world, non-Christians often deny the existence of good and evil and the notion of sin. Yet, non-Christians are often more successful than Christians at representing sin in film.

This may be true because non-Christians are more likely to acknowledge the void within the human soul. French philosopher and mathematician Blaise Pascal wrote, "There is a God-shaped vacuum in the heart of every man which cannot be filled by any created thing, but only by God the Creator, made known through Jesus Christ." C. S. Lewis used the German word *Sehnsucht* to describe a deep, inner longing for the "other." Even such disparate sources as Jean-Paul Sartre and twelve-step recovery programs acknowledge this "God-shaped hole" in our hearts.

We Christians believe this void is the result of original sin, the rift in our union with God, and that our yearning for completion is a sign of our need for redemption, or reunification with God. Yet we are reticent to show this on screen. Our protagonists must be better than good; they are flawless, and inhumanly so. We are afraid that merely depicting sin is an endorsement of sin.

On the other hand, non-Christians may not call sin "sin," but that doesn't mean they don't acknowledge it in their art. They recognize sin as something in our human nature that prevents us from attaining what they might call "self-actualization" or "enlightenment." In the original screenplay for *American Beauty*, protagonist Lester Burnham (Kevin Spacey) sleeps with the object of his desire, the underaged Angela Hayes (Mena Suvari), before he is murdered at the film's finale. Director Sam Mendes had screenwriter Alan Ball rewrite the ending because he felt Lester must be "redeemed" before he dies. Mendes recognized that though Lester believed sleeping with Angela would fulfill him, this was an empty fantasy that would keep him from true fulfillment. Lester's redemption comes when he acknowledges Angela as a person instead of just a fantasy.

Another example is Tim Robbins's *Dead Man Walking*, which recounts the true story of Sister Helen Prejean's attempt to save Matthew Poncelet's soul. In their pivotal jailhouse conversation, she admonishes him to accept responsibility for his role in the deaths of two teenagers: "Matt, redemption isn't some kinda free admission ticket that you get because Jesus paid the price; you gotta participate in your own redemption. You got some work to do."[5] Matthew finally acknowledges his crime and asks for God's forgiveness.

In taking an unflinching look at their characters, these filmmakers came much closer to telling the truth about sin than most Christian filmmakers—even though they didn't call it "sin."

## An Exception to the Rule

There is one exception to my argument that non-Christians make the best Christian films. A particular group of Christians has excelled in its craft during the past century of cinema. This fraternity includes Frank Capra, Francis Ford Coppola, John Ford, Alfred Hitchcock, Martin Scorsese, Andrei Tarkovsky, Lars Von Trier, and Krzysztof Kieslowski. All operate (or operated) in the mainstream rather than sequestering themselves in a subculture, and all came from a Roman Catholic background.

Three tenets of Catholicism informed their craft and equipped them to excel. First, an intuitive understanding of iconography gave them a strong foundation for crafting visual images. Next, they seemed to grasp the incarnational function of art, which allowed them to give tangible form to intangible concepts. Finally, their understanding of the sacramental nature of life helped them relate divine patterns through everyday minutiae. For these reasons, even lapsed Catholic filmmakers, such as Brian De Palma or Federico Fellini, tend to be better equipped to focus on religious themes than practicing evangelicals. This isn't to say that non-Catholic Christian filmmakers are at a complete disadvantage when creating cinema. But the Protestant evangelical emphasis on the primacy of "word" has not allowed us to fully realize our ability to translate the image of God (*imago Dei*) into moving pictures.

From *Places in the Heart* to *The Apostle* to *Dead Man Walking*, secular filmmakers have continually shamed us by treating Christian themes and subject matter with grace and depth, while our filmmakers have been too busy making apocalyptic schlock to notice. If we, as a community, can embrace and learn from what non-Christians are doing with the art form, then perhaps our next generation of filmmakers will be different. They will have to learn to make films for the mainstream, to embrace metaphor and eschew propaganda, and to be more objective observers—to wrestle with tough questions and to portray sin as it really is. If they do not, we will continue to be scandalized by the fact that heathens make the best Christian films.

**Notes**

1. Herbert Lockyer, *All the Parables of the Bible* (Grand Rapids: Zondervan, 1963), 10.

2. Anthony Breznican, review of *Left Behind*, Associated Press, February 2, 2001.

3. Rod Dreher, "Do Fake Boobs Go to Heaven?" *National Review*, February 6, 2001.

4. *The Apostle*, written and directed by Robert Duvall (Los Angeles: October Films, 1997).

5. *Dead Man Walking*, written and directed by Tim Robbins (MGM/UA Home Entertainment Inc.).

# 5    The Divine Image

### Leo Partible

In 1970, Jack Kirby, the co-architect of Marvel Comics along with Stan Lee, stood on the floor of the San Diego Comic-Con in a room of five hundred people and made what was then a startling pronouncement: "This will be the epicenter, not just of the comic book business, but of all forms of entertainment. This is where Hollywood will come to check out the new trends and see what they'll be producing the next year."

Kirby was right. The Comic-Con has become a must for anyone who's anyone in Hollywood. In 2005, over 100,000 packed the Con, including the biggest actors, writers, directors, and producers in the business, there to tout their latest

Filmmaker, singer-songwriter, and comic book creator Leo Partible is the cofounder of DPG Visions, a film production and entertainment company that focuses on developing comic books and graphic novels for film and television. His upcoming projects include *Killer Stunts, Inc.*, *The Trouble with Grrrls*, a sci-fi/fantasy/superhero epic inspired by the works of C. S. Lewis and J. R. R. Tolkien called *Powers & Principalities*, as well as an untitled documentary on Christianity and comic books. Leo wrote the foreword to *Who Needs a Superhero?* and contributed to *The Gospel According to Superheroes: Religion & Pop Culture*.

projects or look for their next ones. And consider this: the X-Men movies have grossed over $700 million worldwide, and the Spider-Man movies a whopping $1.6 billion worldwide, not including DVD and merchandising revenues.

It's no wonder Hollywood is banking on the draw of comic books to hold up the studio tents these days. In 2005 and 2006, Superman, Batman, the Fantastic Four, Wolverine, Hellblazer, Elektra, Ghost Rider, and Sub-Mariner will all get the big-screen treatment. While not technically based on comic books, films such as *The Matrix* trilogy, *The Incredibles*, and *Unbreakable* drew on comics as their main source of inspiration. And then there's the comic book's close cousins, the sci-fi and fantasy genres, which count among their ranks such films as *The Lord of the Rings* trilogy, *Harry Potter*, *Star Wars*, and *Raiders of the Lost Ark*.

The comic book has become central to, if not the center of, our pop culture. And Christians should be thrilled. Comic books and comic-book movies, as well as the sci-fi and fantasy genres, frequently deal with Christian themes and employ Christ figures. *Spider-Man* is a story of responsibility and personal sacrifice. The predominant theme of the X-Men films and comics is the need for tolerance and brotherhood. *The Incredibles* is about the importance of family. And Harry Potter's story, in some ways, parallels the Old Testament hero Daniel (called the "Chief of Magicians").

Yet most Christians have failed to recognize this exciting trend in our culture, much less capitalize on it. Christians have been virtually silent about Spider-Man, X-Men, and the Incredibles. Meanwhile, Christian groups banned the Harry Potter novels, accusing author J. K. Rowling of endorsing witchcraft. (Rowling, a member of the Church of Scotland, frequently employs Christian symbolism in her books.) *A Wrinkle in Time* author Madeleine L'Engle, a devout Christian, has weathered similar attacks.

Christians were once at the forefront of the arts and popular culture. We embraced every new technology, such as the printing press, which we used to make the gospel easily accessible. We elevated art and music to new heights of sophistication during the Renaissance, developing photo-realistic painting and grand symphonies of layered complexity. Until recent times, the church inspired the creation of new forms of music. Blues, jazz, gospel, and rock'n'roll had their roots in the church. The genesis of the motion picture was the "Magic Lantern" presentations that missionaries gave in China.

No longer leaders of artistic innovation, Christians today are on the fringes of the culture. Evangelicalism has stubbornly maintained an emphasis on the verbal and literal, while the rest of society has become increasingly dependent on the visual and metaphorical.

It's no wonder Christians have trouble with comic books and comic-book movies—fantastic, highly metaphorical stories told through visual media. Christians fear that the god-like heroes of these stories are somehow in competition with the God of Scripture. Superpowered beings and supernatural phenomena not clearly stated as originating in the biblical God are seen as false idols and witchcraft.

But Christians have completely missed the metaphorical nature of these stories. In recent history we have limited God's communicative powers and expression to the literal word in our reading of Scripture. We need to realize that the literal word is perhaps the beginning but hardly the full extent of God's communication. The Bible goes beyond simple didacticism, presenting the truth through literary devices such as symbols, metaphors, and allegories. In the Gospels, Christ tells parables and uses hyperbole. In much the same way, good comic book stories use hyperrealism to communicate a universal truth. They present exaggerated representations of human experience that can affirm, teach, and inspire.

I learned how to draw at a very young age. My father says I was barely three when I first picked up a pen. Of course, I was scratching and scribbling at that age. We lived in the Philippines, and I would wander into the rooms of our student boarders, looking for a pen and paper. If I couldn't find any paper, I'd draw on the walls. Or anything flat and white.

Before long, my drawings began to resemble real objects: cars, people, animals. It was during that time I saw my first cartoon on television, a rerun of the sixties' Marvel Comics show *Captain America*. (I still remember the theme song: "When Captain America throws his mighty shield . . . Captain America . . . one, two, three!")

I have my dad to blame for my comic book devotion. He had youthful dreams of drawing comic book heroes, but my grandfather urged him to choose a more "practical" career. So my father became a CPA and immigrated to the United States in the early seventies. While I was growing up in San Francisco, he would still read the occasional comic book. It was from him that I received my first issue of *World's Finest Comics*, a DC Comic book featuring Superman and Batman and their super sons, Superman Jr. and Batman Jr.

I was hooked.

My two brothers and I begged our dad to buy us more from the emporium near our basement apartment off Market Street. He did, and I discovered the world of the superhero. I learned about integrity and the American dream from Superman and Captain America; commitment from Batman; social justice from Green Lantern, Green Arrow, and Daredevil; the importance of family from the Fantastic Four and the X-Men; loyalty and friendship from the Justice League; and sacrifice from Phoenix and Ferro Lad, superheroes who died in the line of duty. I especially identified with Superman as an immigrant, Batman as a perfectionist, and Spider-Man as the underdog.

Later, I would recognize that comic books often depict a Judeo-Christian worldview in subtle ways. Young Jewish and Roman Catholic writers and cartoonists created the comic book industry in the 1930s, when the prevailing worldview was still traditional. The stories reflected the times and the upbringing of their creators. Superheroes characterized essentially biblical values: doing good deeds in secret, a respect for authority, loyalty, patience, kindness, fighting for truth, sacrifice for a friend or a neighbor, rejecting the use of power for personal gain, defending the weak and the powerless, the importance of family, taking a stand for justice. There was an idealistic core to the comic book world that became part and parcel of the medium. The tone of the stories may have grown darker over the years, but their moral heart remains intact. Everyone knows that Superman stands for "Truth, Justice, and the American Way," but even a shadowy vigilante like Batman abides by a strict code not to kill.

This spirit of idealism has translated to the big screen. Long before *Spider-Man* the movie made them famous, comic book fans knew by heart the words: "With great power comes great responsibility."

In the few instances when the film failed to capture the idealism of the source material, comic book fans rejected it. The 1989 Tim Burton production of *Batman* featured a Dark Knight who had no qualms about killing those who got in his way. While the movie did well at the box office, fans complained that this was not the character they had read over the years. When director Chris Nolan restarted the Batman series in 2005 with *Batman Begins*, he made sure the Batman mythos remained intact. As star Christian Bale described the character, "He's attempting to take his pain and his guilt and his anger and the rage and do something good with it, even though his impulses are that he does just want to rage and break bones and do damage."[1]

Another criticism of the comic book has been that it is a child's medium. But just because children's stories are imaginative doesn't mean that all imaginative tales are for children. C. S. Lewis agreed:

> There is a level of sophistication that is beyond even what is considered mature reading. The fantastic or mythical is a mode available at all ages for some readers; for others, at none. At all ages, if it is well used by the author and meets the right reader, it has the same power: to generalize while remaining concrete, to present in palpable form not concepts or even experiences but whole classes of experience, and to throw off irrelevancies. But at its best it can do more; it can give us experiences we can never have and thus, instead of "commenting on life," can add to it.[2]

Is it any wonder that Jesus said, "I tell you the truth, unless you change and become like little children, you will never enter the kingdom of heaven. Therefore, whoever humbles himself like this child is the greatest in the kingdom of heaven" (Matt. 18:3–4).

In a time when the superhero has captured the imagination of so many millions around the world, we must encourage a new generation of renaissance creators, men and women with soaring visions who can tackle the difficult questions.

There are signs that the church is beginning to embrace these means of spreading the gospel. A recent issue of *Christianity Today* reported a change of heart in many churches:

> "We believe the Reformers missed something big," says [Rev. Bruce] Marcey, a doctoral candidate in visual rhetoric at Regent University in Virginia Beach, Va. "When we limit the gospel message to the written and spoken text, we short-circuit

it. We truncate it . . . the soul is moved by more things than the word." Marcey's church is not alone. Across the nation, visual images are fast becoming a part of religious life for millions of Reformed Protestant Christians whose tradition has for centuries regarded pictures with great suspicion. Wariness of the image's power to become an idol, or otherwise deceive a lost soul, has largely given way to confidence in the power of images to reach souls for the good.[3]

The world is in great pain. But, to paraphrase Madeleine L'Engle, "storytelling is the great painkiller." We tell stories to help us remember that someday there will be a better tomorrow, no matter how distant it may seem, and that the biggest dream of all, to live in glory with Christ Jesus forever and ever, will be a reality. Let us present our big dreams to the world, and we can start with the world of the comic book.

**Notes**

1. Rebecca Murray, "Interview with Christian Bale," February 22, 2005, www.about .com.

2. C. S. Lewis, *On Stories: And Other Essays on Literature* (New York: Harcourt, Brace, Jovanovich, 1982).

3. Macdonald G. Jeffrey, "Reformed Protestants No Longer See Images as Idolatrous," *Christianity Today*, December 6, 2004.

# 6     In Defense of the Christian Movie Buff

## James Scott Bell

Before I knew about Jesus, I knew about Will Kane.

Will Kane is the town marshal in the classic movie *High Noon*. Played by Gary Cooper in a role that won him a well-deserved Oscar, Kane is the classic Western hero, the man who stands up against bad men and long odds.

When we first see Kane, he is getting married to a beautiful Quaker woman (Grace Kelly). He's decided to give up his tin star and start a quiet home life. But then he gets the terrible news: Frank Miller, a ruthless killer Kane testified against, has been released from state prison. He's on his way to town on the noon train, where he'll meet with three of his cohorts. Miller has one obsession: to kill Will Kane.

---

James Scott Bell is the best-selling author of *Breach of Promise*, *Deadlock*, *A Greater Glory*, and several other novels. He is a winner of the Christy Award for Excellence in Christian fiction and is currently a fiction columnist for *Writer's Digest* magazine. His book *Plot & Structure* has just been released from Writer's Digest Books. James teaches screenwriting and fiction at numerous writers conferences and at Pepperdine University. His website is www.jamesscottbell.com.

The town leaders urge Kane to take his wife and flee. He hops on a carriage and starts off. He stops just outside town. "I can't do this," he tells his wife. If he runs, Miller will come after them. There will be no rest. He's got to stay in town and face Miller once and for all.

It won't be too hard, he reasons. After all, he's served the town for years, and he'll have no trouble enlisting a posse.

But everybody in town has an excuse not to join Kane. As the clock ticks inexorably toward high noon, Kane realizes he will be alone—and he will almost certainly die.

The climax of the film is one I will not reveal here, because the pleasure in great movies lies in experiencing them first-hand. What I will say is that the film had a profound impact on me as a child, and I'm sure it shaped me in ways I'm not even aware of.

Cut to: twenty years later. I am one of a handful of Christians in the law school I attend. One day a group of students begins to criticize Christianity, and I argue in defense of the historic faith. At once I am besieged on all sides. It would be easy to walk away, but I don't.

Was it Will Kane who inspired me to stay? Maybe. I was wild about movies as a kid, and after I became a Christian that passion did not leave me. And movie heroes—from Robin Hood to William Wallace—continue to move me.

I am an unabashed movie buff, but that term, modified by the adjective "Christian," has not been common in the short history of motion pictures.

Movies came of age in the twentieth century at the same time a monumental fight was being waged—not World War I but the fight of *The Fundamentals*. This series of booklets, issued beginning around 1910, defended biblical Christianity against a wave of liberal theology and modernism in America. It also viewed certain amusements with a jaundiced eye.

The general editor of *The Fundamentals*, R. A. Torrey, was dean of the Bible Institute of Los Angeles (BIOLA) and preacher at the famous Church of the Open Door. Torrey came out strongly against movies as a pastime for Christians. His arguments were not reactionary; indeed, they contain warnings all Christians ought to consider.

Above all, Torrey criticized movies for the immoral lifestyle many in the industry lead. Ministering in Los Angeles, he witnessed countless examples of Hollywood's dark side, such as the Fatty Arbuckle scandal of 1921. During a debauch in San Francisco, a young actress, Virginia Rappe, ended up dead in the portly celebrity's hotel suite. Witnesses testified about all-night drinking and Arbuckle's rough handling of Miss Rappe. Arbuckle was arrested and charged with murder. Eventually he was exonerated, but not without fatal damage to his film career.

Torrey also thought the moral content of most films was irreconcilable with the Christian life. For these reasons, he strongly advised Christians not to attend movies.

Thus, for decades afterward, one of the marks of fundamentalism would be a distrust and avoidance of movies. This became part of fundamentalism's growing culture of separation. Though mainline Protestant denominations did not share this separatist strain or view movies with the same unease, similar ideas would rise out of their ranks.

But with movies and television having become so pervasive over the past century, many Christians are finally asking if there is a place—indeed, an imperative—for the Christian movie buff.

Movies are a part of our cultural syntax. They help shape our language and our conversations. Recall how the Matrix trilogy provoked a rich discussion of transcendent things. This is just the sort of cultural conversation we need to be having, but we can't participate if we are not engaged with culture.

The need for Christians with a passion for film goes beyond the need for "keeping our finger on the pulse." Like all great art, great movies can be a healing balm for us as individuals and as a society. God is the author of beauty, and when we experience beauty in the form of art, a doorway opens through which God can enter into our lives. Movies can inspire.

They can also teach. We all know Jesus taught in parables and that parables essentially paint word pictures. Jesus told vivid tales using the things of his day—farmers, widows, judges, camels, birds, and the like. These pictures moved his audience toward a greater understanding of the kingdom of God. Moving pictures can do the same for today's audiences.

Finally, Christian movie buffs can encourage fellow Christians to make better films. In Woody Allen's *Stardust Memories*, Woody plays Sandy Bates, a successful director of film comedies. Sandy decides he wants to get serious, so he makes an art film, which is immediately panned. The critics say they used to like his films, particularly the early funny ones. Sandy is in despair. He wants to make a statement that is important to the world.

A spaceship with super-intelligent aliens has landed in a field and is about to take off. Sandy races out to them.

**Sandy**: Wait a minute! Don't go! I've got some questions.

**Og**: We can't breathe your air.

**Sandy**: You guys gotta tell me, why is there so much human suffering?

**Og**: This is unanswerable.

**Sandy**: Is there a God?

**Og**: You're asking the wrong questions.

**Sandy**: Look, here's my point. If nothing lasts, why am I bothering to make films, or do anything for that matter?

**Og**: We enjoy your films. Particularly the early funny ones.

**Sandy**: But the human condition is so discouraging.

**Og**: There are some nice moments too.

**Sandy**: But shouldn't I stop making movies and do something that counts, like helping blind people or becoming a missionary or something?

**Og**: Let me tell you, you're not the missionary type. You'd never last. And incidentally, you're also not Superman, you're a comedian. You want to do mankind a real service? Tell funnier jokes.[1]

But what of the concerns that Torrey and fundamentalism expressed about movies? Are movies fundamentally dangerous and "irreconcilable to a Christian life"? The answer is the same for any choice a Christian makes.

First, "put on the full armor of God so that you can take your stand against the devil's schemes" (Eph. 6:11). As Paul explains, this armor is made up of a firm belief in absolute Truth; a dedication to carrying the gospel everywhere; complete faith; the covering of salvation in Christ; being rooted in the Word of God; and prayer. Without these, the Christian, movie buff or not, is at risk of being seduced by the power of the cinematic art form and losing a healthy critical perspective.

Second, "whether you eat or drink or whatever you do, do it all for the glory of God" (1 Cor. 10:31). Whether Christians are watching films or making films, their primary concern must be the glory of God. If cinema ever becomes the sole, or even highest, concern for the Christian, then cinema becomes an idol. The question must constantly be asked, What can I do for God with what I know?

Finally, "'everything is permissible'—but not everything is beneficial. 'Everything is permissible'—but not everything is constructive" (1 Cor. 10:23). There will be times when the Christian movie buff will skip a film for spiritual reasons. Not every movie is beneficial or constructive. That is an individual determination, based on wisdom, and is not subject to a legalistic rule. But we have this promise: "If any of you lacks wisdom, he should ask God, who gives generously to all without finding fault, and it will be given to him" (James 1:5).

American film history is rich and varied, and the Christian-movie-buff-to-be has a lifetime of viewing pleasure awaiting him or her. (Foreign films are another universe of movie experience, beyond the scope of this chapter.)

Of course, there are some standards all movie mavens must know, like *Casablanca*, *Citizen Kane*, *The Wizard of Oz*, and *Gone with the Wind*. To that list, I would add the following:

*Mr. Smith Goes to Washington* (1939)—Starring James Stewart, Jean Arthur, and Claude Raines, the film tells the story of Jefferson Smith, a naive scout leader who is tapped by a political machine to become a puppet U.S. senator. But when he finds out the real score and tries to stand up against the machine, he's hit with everything they've got.

The movie's theme is summed up in something Jefferson Smith's father once told him. "Sometimes lost causes are the only ones worth fighting for."

Unabashedly American, *Smith* is the quintessential Frank Capra film, even more so than *It's a Wonderful Life*.

*Twelve Angry Men* (1957)—Directed by Sidney Lumet and starring Henry Fonda and eleven other fine actors (most notably Lee J. Cobb and Jack Warden), this classic "one man against the crowd" film is a legal mystery with social themes aplenty. See it for its tremendous acting and its ability to tell multiple stories without ever leaving the jury room.

*On the Waterfront* **(1954)**—This classic from director Elia Kazan and writer Budd Schulberg has what I think is the greatest performance by an actor ever put on film. Marlon Brando plays Terry Malloy, a pug fighter now working for the mob. This immensely moving drama of one man's awakening from animal existence through the love of woman features plenty of fine performances (Lee J. Cobb, Karl Malden, Eva Marie Saint) and has the famous cab scene between Rod Steiger and Marlon Brando. "I coulda had class! I coulda been a contender! I coulda been *somebody*."

As a plus, it is also about standing up against evil no matter what the cost.

*Shane* **(1953)**—I agree with the great director Sam Peckinpah that *Shane* is the greatest Western ever. But to me, calling *Shane* a Western is like calling *Moby Dick* a fish story. What makes *Shane* a classic is that you find new things in every viewing. Indeed, I think you need five or six viewings, minimum, to see the richness of it.

On first viewing, naturally, one sees the main story—a rather spare tale about homesteaders versus cattle ranchers. That's as it should be. It's a good, timeless story, well told.

But there is so much more going on.

First, appreciate the filmmaking artistry. Every frame is perfect. Watch the way the actors and mountains and props are framed to obtain specific effects. Director George Stevens used a telephoto lens to achieve that incredible reality of the Grand Tetons out in the backyard. (No Western, and few movies before or since, has had such striking imagery. The movie that has come closest to achieving this effect is Ford's *Monument Valley*.)

The film is a Christian allegory (even more explicit in the novel). The devil makes an appearance in the form of

Jack Palance, whose stunning portrayal earned him a Best Supporting Actor nomination.

*Hail the Conquering Hero* (1944)—This, the finest film of director/writer Preston Sturges (who flashed like a comet across the Hollywood heavens in the early forties), is on the surface a simple screwball comedy. Woodrow Lafayette Pershing Truesmith (Eddie Bracken), the son of a World War I hero, has been released by the Marines because of a hay fever problem. Ashamed to go home, he makes the acquaintance of seven Marines on furlough led by a crusty but benign sergeant (William Demarest). The sergeant was with Woodrow's father when he was killed. He and his buddies hatch a plan to pass Woodrow off as a hero to his small town.

The plot unfolds with typical Sturges energy. But underneath it is a story about duty owed to home and family, and the unbreakable bonds of friendship. The last shot in the film is one of the most perfect in movie history, explaining everything that happened with one simple image.

*Duck Soup* (1933)—The best of the Marx Brothers films, this also remains a trenchant political satire, timeless in its way. It is also a reminder of how dreadful so many "comedies" are these days. The secret of Marx was great writing mixed with perfect timing and delivery.

Watch for the often-imitated mirror scene, in which Harpo, dressed like Groucho, tries to mimic Groucho's every move in an open doorway.

*The Best Years of Our Lives* (1946)—Classic Americana is on display in the story of three vets returning from World War II. Frederic March earned a Best Actor Oscar, and Harold Russell, a Navy vet who had lost both hands in the war, took home the Best Supporting Actor statuette. Dana Andrews, never better, plays the role of the third vet.

In addition, this film has what I consider to be one of the two most perfect film scores ever (the other being from *To Kill a Mockingbird*).

These are just a few favorites from this movie buff. You will of course compile your own list of favorites, but don't be content with a single viewing. Digging into your favorite movies, finding out what it is that moves you, is the great enterprise of the movie buff. And the themes you uncover, the truths you find, will turn your viewing pleasure, ultimately, into a joyful pilgrimage of discovery.

---

**Notes**

1. *Stardust Memories*, written and directed by Woody Allen (UA/MGM Home Entertainment, 1980).

# 7      The World's Most Influential Mission Field

## Karen and Jim Covell

Do you consider Hollywood a mission field?

For a documentary short I produced called "The Hollywood Crisis," churchgoing Christians were asked this same question. Their answers were unanimous: "No!" "Absolutely not!" "No way!" etc. And yet, every day, young Christians are coming to Hollywood, convinced that God has called them to be missionaries in the entertainment industry.

Sure, Hollywood doesn't look like a traditional mission field. Most people in the entertainment industry live in nice homes, drive fancy cars, and have plenty to eat. But spiritually, they are starving. Only about 2 percent of media professionals

Karen Covell is a television producer and director of the Hollywood Prayer Network (Hollywoodprayernetwork.org). Her producing credits include *Headliners and Legends with Matt Lauer* for MSNBC and *America's Throwaway Children*. Jim Covell's musical scores range from feature films to television series and specials (JamesCovell.com). He has several commissioned orchestral works and composed and conducted for the London Symphony Orchestra. Jim and Karen are coauthors with Victorya Michaels Rogers of *How to Talk About Jesus Without Freaking Out* and *The Day I Met God*.

go to church or synagogue. Hollywood is an isolated society, ignorant of—and often hostile to—Christianity.

Hollywood is not just a mission field, it is the world's most influential mission field. The media shapes the hearts and minds of people around the world. Any foreign missionary will tell you that the greatest Western influence on their people group is the American media. If we minister to Hollywood, we will be ministering to the whole world.

But Christians long ago turned their backs on Hollywood, deeming it Sodom and Gomorrah, a cesspool of sin and skin beyond redemption. For most Christians, Hollywood is not a mission field but an enemy who must be destroyed (or, just as bad, Satan's pit, a place to avoid at all costs).

This attitude has not only discouraged those of us already doing God's work here in Hollywood, but it has also dissuaded young people of faith from coming here. Many of these young people believe God is calling them here to be missionaries, but because their parents, pastors, and friends bear such fear and hatred toward Hollywood, they have stayed away.

Meanwhile, all this talk of Hollywood's depravity has only deepened the rift between the church and the entertainment industry. It's no wonder that when Christians do appear in the movies or on TV, they're portrayed as hateful, judgmental people.

And then there are the boycotts, the threats to not buy this product or watch that TV show because we don't like what we see. As a church, we should have learned by now that these tactics don't work. Can you imagine marching through the villages of the Massai tribe, denouncing their public circumcision rituals and threatening never again to buy their bracelets unless they stop? Jim and I have never met a person in Hollywood who has become a Christian because of a boycott.

Perhaps it's time we see Hollywood less like Sodom and more like Nineveh.

In the book of Jonah, God commands Jonah to go to Nineveh to bring its people back into the fold. Jonah, however, hates the Ninevites. Not wanting to see them forgiven, he turns his back on them and flees. From inside the belly of a whale, Jonah learns to accept God's will and put aside his personal feelings. He goes to Nineveh, and they hear and accept the Word of God.

There is hope for Hollywood. But like Nineveh needed Jonah, Hollywood needs *our* help. So what can we do?

First, we can pray for Hollywood. A Christian pastor once said, "Prayer is not preparation for the greater work; prayer is the greater work." If people of faith outside of Hollywood can replace their anger, fear, and frustration toward the media with prayer, and if Christians in Hollywood commit all that we do and say to prayer, we will, without question, see God redeem the land.

There are a few established prayer efforts that anyone can join. Mastermedia International publishes a Media Leader Prayer Calendar that lists influential people in the media to pray for every day of the year. The Hollywood Prayer Network unifies Christians around the world to pray for Hollywood and the people in it. HPN offers a monthly email newsletter listing people and shows to pray for. Through our "I to I" program, HPN finds Christians outside Hollywood to pray for specific Christians in the industry. HPN now has over four hundred of these prayer partnerships, with the goal of providing every Christian in the media with another Christian to pray for them. We encourage Christians to join the global prayer effort at www.hollywoodprayernetwork.org and www.mastermediaintl.org.

A second thing Christians can do to acknowledge Hollywood as a mission field is send more missionaries. We should encourage talented people who are grounded in their faith to come work here in the entertainment industry.

Hollywood, however, is a difficult place to earn a living, and many people leave broke and discouraged because they didn't have any support as they tried to survive on the "front lines." Pastors and churches should keep track of those in their ranks who decide to move to Hollywood, so that they can offer them prayers and even financial support as they get their feet planted.

Parents should not be afraid to send their artistic sons or daughters to Hollywood. The church lifts up and celebrates young people who feel called to go to Africa, China, and the far reaches of India. Are these places any safer or more blessed by God than Hollywood? The Los Angeles Film Studies Center offers a semester in Hollywood program to students through the Council for Christian Colleges and Universities. Young people have the opportunity to intern with companies like Miramax, Universal, and Sony while living in a supportive Christian community. Is this any less valuable or holy than learning how to farm with a family in China?

The third way to impact Hollywood is for Christians in Hollywood to be bolder in sharing their faith with nonbelieving co-workers and peers. Jim and I discovered years ago that God was indeed answering our prayers and bringing more Christians here, but they were hiding their faith in the closet. They were afraid to talk about their faith to non-Christian bosses, co-workers, and friends. They believed that if anyone found out that they were Christians, they might not work again. They feared being shunned, or even persecuted.

The good news is that this kind of discrimination is rare in Hollywood today. Media professionals see us as confusing, sometimes annoying, and definitely odd, but mostly they find us fascinating. Most non-Christians in Hollywood have never met a real live "normal" Christian. And because they are hungry for truth and peace, they are often curious to know what Christianity is all about. Christians in Hollywood have the unique opportunity to be salt and light, to be the bearers of Good News. It takes boldness and a maturity of faith, but the opportunities are waiting for us.

Jim and I share a passion for training and encouraging other Christians in Hollywood to talk about Jesus "without freaking out." We have been teaching classes in our home for over fourteen years on how to be bold, confident, and yet sensitive and loving in sharing our faith with others. When our friend and agent, Victorya Michaels Rogers, started teaching with us, the three of us decided to write a book: *How to Talk About Jesus Without Freaking Out.* We have seen incredible miracles as Christians step out of their comfort zones and talk about Jesus in Hollywood.

One of the most surprising ways that I got to share my faith was when I was hired to work as associate producer for the West Coast production team on *Headliners and Legends with Matt Lauer*, a show that airs on MSNBC. Initially, I was excited about the opportunity. Then I discovered my first assignment was to be a part of the team producing a one-hour profile on Hugh Hefner, the creator of *Playboy* magazine. I was so disappointed. When I complained to Jim about the assignment, he reminded me that working with Hugh Hefner is *exactly* why we are here. He suggested that we start praying and that I talk to my producer, Rick, to see if we could approach the project from a different perspective. I walked into Rick's office the next day, praying that he would have the ears to hear my ideas. To my surprise, as I started talking about the project, Rick immediately told me how disappointed he was at the assignment as well. After receiving it, he said, he went straight home and called his pastor. I was floored. I had no idea he was a Christian. Rick went on to relate how his pastor told him he couldn't turn down this assignment. Someone was going to do the story, the pastor had said, and if Rick turned it down, it would likely be done as a standard puff piece. This was an opportunity to really dig deeper into why Hugh Hefner became the man he is.

We thanked God for bringing us together and proceeded to investigate Hugh's upbringing and spiritual background. Our journey culminated in a miraculous interview. Hugh described how he had been brought up by legalistic parents who never told him they loved him. His mother never hugged or kissed him, he said, because of her fear of germs. He found security and solace in his treasured "bunny blanket," the edges of which were framed by little bunny rabbits. His greatest loss, he said, was the day his puppy died while lying on his blanket. Immediately after burying the puppy, his mother burned the blanket. Hugh concluded that he thinks he's still just a little boy trying to find love.

When the interview was done, everyone in the room was completely silent. Finally, Hugh's PR woman said, "This wasn't an interview; it was a therapy session." God had visited that room and touched the hearts of all who were there. And it all came from prayer and our willingness to be used by the Lord in the entertainment industry. We know of other Christians who have shared their faith with Hugh since the interview. This could not have been possible if there weren't Christians working in this mission field and reaching out one-on-one with God's love.

We also know of a network TV executive who became a Christian through his relationship with a missionary here. The executive embraced Jesus in the midst of developing an "edgy" sitcom for his network. Once his heart had changed, he looked at his script and started changing things. He cut and added until the script became impossible to produce. "Once I became one of you born-againers," he said, "I just couldn't write that stuff anymore." When his heart changed, his writing changed.

How do we change the media? We change the hearts of the people creating the media.

The most effective way to share our faith in the entertainment industry is to communicate our worldview to our co-workers. But sometimes it takes creativity. Jim, as a composer, does not often get the opportunity to express his faith through his music, but he always gets to share his faith with his musicians.

A few years ago Jim went to England to score a film with the London Symphony. He brought with him a wonderful book called *The Spiritual Lives of the Great Composers*. During the recording session, he read excerpts from the book that expressed how important God was in the lives of composers—from Bach to Stravinsky. At the end of the session, he gave each member of the orchestra a copy. The musicians were thrilled and shocked by the gesture. Though they were late to a session with Paul McCartney, each of them waited in line, with their instruments under their arms, to get their book and shake Jim's hand. "My goodness," remarked a trombonist, "I didn't know musicians had spiritual lives."

By praying for Hollywood, building up the body of missionaries in Hollywood, and sharing our faith in Hollywood, we will see more changes there.

We know many Christians just want Hollywood to make cleaner, less offensive entertainment. But they must understand that the only way to change the movies and TV shows coming out of Hollywood is to change the hearts of the people producing them. We must stop trying to make Hollywood act like Christians, via protests and boycotts, and start focusing on them becoming Christians.

On the final page of his book *Roaring Lambs*, Bob Briner challenges us with these words:

> I recall numerous missionary conventions where young people would be challenged to commit themselves to missions.... That same spirit needs to prevail when we think about sending our children into the rough and tumble world of television, film, and other culture-shaping careers. These are the

new missionaries that have a shot at turning our nation back toward God. I envision a whole new generation of roaring lambs who will lay claim to these careers with the same vigor and commitment that sent men like Hudson Taylor to China. Will you dare share that vision with me?[1]

Do you believe that God sent his Son into the world not to condemn Hollywood but so that Hollywood might be saved through him? Then share the vision with us here. Perhaps, just like Jonah, you'll be surprised by a receptive audience. And God will indeed revive our land.

---

**Notes**

1. Bob Briner, *Roaring Lambs* (Grand Rapids: Zondervan, 1995).

# 8     So You Wanna Come
# to Hollywood

## Janet Scott Batchler

So it's come to this, has it? You wanna come to Hollywood.

Maybe all your life you felt deep down inside that the Oscars and the Emmys were really important, even though you could never justify why, even to yourself.

Maybe you had ideas—really good ideas—and no one in your small-town high school understood what you were talking about and thought you were a tad weird.

Perhaps you watched something on TV and said, "I could do that." Or "I wish I could do that." Or you watched something on TV or in the movies and got mad. Mad at the quality, mad at the message, mad at both.

With her husband and writing partner, Lee, Janet Scott Batchler's feature credits include the blockbuster *Batman Forever* for Warner Bros. and *My Name Is Modesty* for Miramax— an intro to the "female James Bond" based on the well-known English novels and comic strip. Their adventure movie *Smoke and Mirrors* is currently in development with Michael Douglas and Catherine Zeta-Jones set to star. The Batchlers have written action-adventure scripts for every studio and are in demand as speakers, with Janet currently teaching screenwriting for the UCLA film school.

Whatever sparked it, the bottom line is you think God is calling you, like a Moses, to the strangest of strange lands: Hollywood. But are you sure it's the voice of God? How do you know if you're supposed to go to Hollywood?

Well, I can't speak to whether that was God on the phone. But I can tell you why you *should* come to Hollywood—and why you shouldn't. And I can tell you some things you'd better pack if you're going to make the trip.

### Three Good Reasons to Come to Hollywood

*Do consider coming to Hollywood if that's who God made you to be.*

In the musical *A Chorus Line*, Cassie sings, "God, I'm a dancer. A dancer dances."

If God truly put you on this earth to dance, it would be a sin if you didn't do it. A dancer dances. An actor acts. A writer writes. A designer designs.

For some of us, Hollywood is simply where we belong. Our talents, our desires, everything about us screams that this is home.

What that often means, of course, is that where you came from doesn't feel like "home." You don't fit in. People there don't understand what makes you tick and what you think is important. You long for kindred spirits, for a place to belong.

Now, the irony here is that coming to Hollywood will not satisfy your yearning to belong. You'll come face to face with more rejection than you ever thought existed in the world—guaranteed. But somehow, if you're meant to be here, none of that will matter. Just having the opportunity to be the person God meant you to be—even if no one ever sees the results—can be enough.

*Do consider coming to Hollywood because you love the end product.*

I know a guy who grew up in love with sitcoms. He inhaled them. He memorized them. He can reel off cast lists, sing opening credits, win every trivia game.

I know another guy who loves being behind a film camera. Even if he didn't get paid for it, he insists, even if he had to work as a waiter to pay the bills, he'd spend every spare minute of time shooting film. He loves it that much.

Maybe you love your craft that much. You spend your weekends drawing cartoons just for the fun of it. You act in the dumbest church skit. You'd rather sit at your computer writing than anything else. Who cares if you get paid? Who cares if you get noticed? Just getting to do it is fulfilling.

Or maybe you just love being part of a huge vision and helping it come to reality. You might never have the big vision yourself; you might not view yourself as particularly artistic. But you can type, you can organize, you can crunch numbers—and if you're part of "putting on a show," somehow those mundane activities seem more special, more important.

Of course, you can be part of an artistic vision in places other than Hollywood. Maybe your contribution to culture will be to write or act in a *good* church skit (a great gift in itself!). But loving the end product of Hollywood can be a good reason to think about making the move—and it may be a prerequisite.

*Do consider coming to Hollywood because you love the people here.*

I once met the receptionist for one of the nastiest, slimiest, most vulgar producers in Hollywood. A guy who treats everyone like trash. And this receptionist truly loved him. "I know what everyone says about him," she told me, "but he's really the sweetest guy." It wasn't that the receptionist, who was a Christian, didn't see her boss's flaws. Believe me, she did. But God had given her a vision of who her boss was

93

made to be; of what God was in him that made him lovable in spite of his flaws.

This receptionist was right where God wanted her to be: in a dead-end job, working for a guy who'll never give her a promotion or even a raise! Could God actually want us to be in a position where others are more important than we are? Where our real job is to help the people around us be who God has called them to be?

Of course he could. And in Hollywood, we need Christians who feel called to love the people here. And, make no mistake, it can be hard to love people whose lifestyles we disapprove of. *Those sinners!* we might think to ourselves. *If we hang out with them, people will think we're like them. And we can't have that.*

It can be hard to love people who are, frankly, unlovable. People like the nasty producer I mentioned. Or people who are manipulative, selfish, and power hungry.

But all of these folks need to be loved. And if Christians won't do it, who will?

We need Christians in Hollywood, in fact, simply to show the people here what love looks like. The nonbelievers in town don't want to hear dogma, they don't want to hear how rotten you think their lifestyle is—but they do want to be loved.

When nonbelievers looked at the early church, they said, "Behold, how they love one another." We sing, "They'll know we are Christians by our love."

If you can look at Hollywood types and love them wholeheartedly and unashamedly, then please do come to Hollywood!

But while you're looking at your own reasons to make the move, we have to take a moment to consider some other motivations.

94

## Five Reasons Not to Come to Hollywood

*Don't come to Hollywood because you want to be rich and famous.*
Christians, sadly, seem to want fame and fortune as much as everyone else. We practice our Oscar speeches during the commercials. We make our lists of who we'll thank. God, of course, at the head of the list—we want to be "witnesses," after all. We envision our names in the credits, our faces on the screen. I know of a Christian who said he wanted to win an Oscar so he could "be humble before a billion people."

If you're seeking fame and fortune, you're seeking your own glory instead of God's. It's that simple. And you are bound for bitter disappointment.

Try this: ask God *not* to give you success until you're ready to handle it in a way that glorifies him. It's a scary prayer, but until you're ready to pray it (and mean it), don't come to Hollywood.

*Don't come to Hollywood because you want to be loved.*
"You like me! You really, really like me!" We've all laughed at Sally Field's reaction to winning her second Oscar, but frankly, she showed a level of honesty and vulnerability that's not often seen in Hollywood.

Many people come to Hollywood because they want to prove something to their parents, to their brothers or sisters, or to themselves. One award-winning actress once told me, "Well, of course the only reason anyone becomes an actor is because their parents didn't love them enough."

But you already *are* loved. You are loved by the King of the Universe, who gave up his throne for you. If we saw that story line in a movie, we'd know we were seeing true love. But we don't always see it in our own lives.

No one will ever love you more than God Almighty already loves you. No audience, no fan club, no groupies. And God will not love you more than he already does if you come to

Hollywood and become a success. And neither will anyone back home.

*Don't come to Hollywood because you want to be a success for the Lord.* "I want to sell this script so I can glorify the Lord." "I want to be a big star because then I'd really have a public platform to praise the Lord." It sounds so spiritual. But it's only the Hollywood Dream wrapped up in religious platitudes.

Funny how we want to pick and choose how and where we'll serve God. We want the first part of the list in Hebrews 11, the story of the people who:

> conquered kingdoms, administered justice, and gained what was promised; who shut the mouths of lions, quenched the fury of the flames, and escaped the edge of the sword; whose weakness was turned to strength; and who became powerful in battle and routed foreign armies . . . received back their dead by resurrection.

But we don't want to keep going down the chapter; we don't want to be one of those who:

> were tortured . . . faced jeers and flogging, while still others were chained and put in prison . . . were stoned . . . sawed in two . . . put to death by the sword . . . went about in sheepskins and goatskins, destitute, persecuted and mistreated . . .

Maybe God will call you to Hollywood, call you to be a "success" according to the definition of the world. But that's his call to make. And we don't get to choose which half of the Hebrews 11 list we end up on.

*Don't come to Hollywood because you want power.*

Hollywood is a place that attracts people who want power.

But power is a dangerous thing. Few people are equipped to handle the kind of power wielded by those at the top of the Hollywood food chain. Maybe you will be one of them. I can pretty much guarantee, however, that you won't be ready to wield that kind of power the moment you set foot in town.

As Christians, we are to be servants, following our Lord, who came as a servant. As Matthew 20:28 says, "The Son of Man did not come to be served, but to serve." Remember, God didn't call Joseph to *be* Pharaoh, he called him to *serve* Pharaoh.

Are you ready to be a servant? Are you ready to pay your dues? You say you'd rather skip all that and move straight to a position of power and influence? Then how will anyone even know you're a Christian?

*Don't come to Hollywood because you want to pursue a moral agenda.*

Yes, many people in Hollywood pursue lifestyles that can hardly be considered godly, according to anyone's standards. Yes, the place is chock full of unrepentant sinners. But look around your home church. There's a place that's full of sinners too.

Sadly, many in Hollywood expect an attitude of moral superiority from Christians, the attitude of the Pharisee who prayed to himself: "God, I thank you that I am not like other men" (Luke 18:11).

Instead of showing them how "superior" we are, let's surprise them. Come with an attitude of love, come with an attitude of service—and let them try to figure *that* out!

"Wait a minute," you say. "I'm no Pharisee! But I'm truly grieved by the sins emanating from Hollywood." Here's an attitude test for you: are you praying for the people in Hollywood with an attitude of love, wanting what God wants for them, praying for good for them? If you are, thank you. We all need those prayers!

## Packing for the Journey

So now you've thought and prayed deeply over your motivations for coming to Hollywood. You've tested your desires. And you think you're ready to make the move, take the leap.

But what should you pack for the journey?

I'm not talking about sunscreen here—though you certainly will need some. I'm talking about attitudes and attributes that will make it possible for you to survive in Hollywood without crashing and burning. Take a look at the following list and see how many you can check off. (If the answer is "Not that many," please think twice. Maybe you should save yourself a lot of grief and pain—I mean that quite seriously—and bloom where you're already planted.)

### *Talent*

So you make videos for your church. You sang in the talent show in high school. You write a Christmas newsletter that's the envy of your whole list. And everyone always says how talented you are.

But Hollywood is the big leagues. Lots of people are fine baseball players in Little League. Quite a few play with distinction in high school. Some keep playing in college. A few even make it to the minors. But only a *very* few get into the major leagues.

We all love to deceive ourselves. We think we're much more talented than we are. Or, sadly, we think we're far less talented than we are. Or we think that because we're Christians and God is on our side, talent doesn't matter.

Talent does matter. A lot. That's why it's at the head of the list. Are you talented enough at what you do for Hollywood? You may not really find out till you get here. But you will need to have a realistic assessment of your talents at every step of the way.

Someone once asked Steve Martin for his advice on how to make it in showbiz, looking for the secret, the hidden password. Mr. Martin's brilliant answer? "Be so good they can't ignore you."

### *A Desire to Serve Other People*

Unless you're well-born into the business, you will have to pay your dues. And they may take a lot longer to pay than you expect. Are you ready for eight years of working at a job you don't love? Ten years? It could take that long to get your break.

Are you willing to work in a subordinate position? To be an assistant? A gopher? To work hard, earn little, and let someone else get the glory?

We knew someone who, right out of film school, got a job in the mail room at a major agency. Now, a mail room job is pure hell. Cruel treatment, minimal pay, horrible hours, brainless work, constant blame. But at the end of it, if you survive, you know all about the business, you have comrades who will do anything for you, and you have begun a network of connections that will serve you well the rest of your career. No wonder mail room jobs are hard to get.

So this guy we knew got one of these prized, horrid jobs. And after a couple of months, he quit. He was too good, too smart, too talented, he explained to us, to pick up other people's dry cleaning.

You know what? It wasn't that he was too good. It was that he was too proud. And his career, not surprisingly, went absolutely nowhere.

We, as Christians, know that we are always servants. So we should have the best attitudes around. Sure, it's a challenge. But if anyone can meet that challenge, it should be us. Shouldn't it?

### *Faith*

Do you know what you believe? Do you know why you believe it?

I hope so, because your faith will be tested in Hollywood in every way possible—from the temptation to just sort of not mention that you're a Christian, to outright attacks and mockery of what you believe.

People will ask you to compromise. People will lie to you. People will insult your God. Is your faith strong enough to handle these situations?

You will also go through times when it seems as if God has abandoned you. It's so easy to believe that God loves you when you have a steady paycheck, a pretty home, people who love and support you all around. But take those away and see if your faith stands strong. Will your faith stretch to meet these situations?

### *Fortitude*

It will take you years to break in, and more years to reach the level of career you're now dreaming of. If you ever reach it, that is.

Can you persevere for all those years? Do you have the patience to wait?

And do you have the courage to face up to all the disappointments? All the rejections? The sheer bravery to get back up after being slapped to the ground again and again, and say, "Okay, I'll try again. Better this time."

### *A Good Learning Curve*

To quote Peter Guber, "This is a business with no rules—but you break them at your peril."[1] No matter where you're coming from, you'll have a whole new set of rules to learn.

Sure, you'll make mistakes. And you'll get second chances. But if you can't learn from your mistakes—and learn quickly—you won't survive.

### *Love for People in the Biz*

Especially if you grew up in a warm, sheltering Christian environment, you will probably meet people in Hollywood unlike those you are used to.

Can you get along with people who feng shui their offices, seek advice from psychics, and take the astrology column seriously? How about with militant gays who think you're the enemy? Or people who lead a life of sexual recklessness and substance abuse? Or people who've never set foot in a Wal-Mart and think nothing of spending eight hundred dollars on a pair of shoes?

If people don't like you, you won't work. And if you send out a vibe that says you don't like them, well, chances are they won't like you.

Of course, loving these people is much better than merely liking them. And as Christians, we should have a head start on that. Shouldn't we?

### *Wisdom*

So many Christians come to Hollywood with "kick me" on their backs. They're well-meaning, sweet, kind . . . and flat-out naive. "The naive man believes everything," warns Proverbs 14:15.

When God offered Solomon anything he wanted, Solomon had his chance to be rich and famous. But he chose wisdom instead. You need to make the same choice if you are to survive.

You need God's wisdom to understand the various agendas at work around you. To understand who's your friend, who's your ally, who's your enemy. To know what projects to pursue. What projects to quit. "You got to know when to hold 'em, know when to fold 'em . . . ."

Seek wisdom if you want to come to Hollywood.

### *A Hunger to Improve*

So many Christians come to town with a good level of talent—and never get any better. Don't let that be you.

You must be willing—hungry—to get better. You will never fully master your craft. You may have to learn radically new technology, jumping from linear editing to nonlinear, from film to video, from digital video to high definition. The better you get at your craft, the more you'll discover how much there is to learn and master. Which is great, because it means you'll never get bored!

Hollywood is not a place for the lazy.

### *Hope*

Life in Hollywood is a life of disappointment. There are hundreds of qualified people out after every job. I can't imagine anything more discouraging than showing up at an audition and looking around to see fifty other people who look like you, sound like you, are dressed better than you, and probably went to school with the casting director.

Can you walk into that situation and hang on to your hope? Can you take the inevitable rejections and simply say, "Okay, move on," without feeling personally devastated? (Okay, I admit, it takes some practice. But you'll have plenty of chances.)

"Our hope is built on nothing less / Than Jesus' blood and righteousness . . ."[2] Most of the folks in Hollywood build their hope on far less than that!

### *Energy*

It takes a lot of work and a single-minded focus to break in to the industry. This is one of the reasons younger people have an easier time: they've got the energy and they've got the lack of commitments elsewhere that allows them to commit fully to the task ahead of them.

"[Make] the most of every opportunity," Paul tells us, "because the days are evil" (Eph. 5:16). The days are evil if only because they keep on passing, and suddenly you wake up and realize you've been here twelve years and you're no farther along than when you started. Make the most of your energy while you have it.

Your job may also be physically demanding in ways you don't expect. Many directors start strenuous workout schedules as part of their prep before a movie starts, because they know how tough it's going to be physically. Women directors warn each other, "Wear comfortable shoes," because they know the day will come when they'll be so tired they can't put one foot in front of the other. Billy Crystal once said in an interview that he had decided not to host the Oscars that particular year because he needs five months to prepare and to get physically in shape—for one night's work!

### Commitment to a Church

There are lots of great churches in Los Angeles. And there are lots of great reasons to skip church—the beach, the mountains, brunch, the Sunday paper, sleeping in, work . . .

But if you don't make a commitment to a particular body of believers and then honor that commitment at every opportunity, your faith *will* falter. Guaranteed.

And we're talking a real commitment here. Not church-hopping from one place to another because you aren't happy with the selection of members of the opposite sex at your given church. Make a commitment. Join a church. Get plugged in to the Christian community in Hollywood. And show up.

### *A Way to Earn Money*

L.A. is not the cheapest place in America to live. (Though it's not the most expensive, either. People from back East often marvel at how cheap our heating bills are, for instance!)

Can you make enough money to pay rent? For how long? Do you have a "day job"? Skills that you can use to get one?

Lots of people come out with enough money saved up to last, say, six months, assuming they'll get their big break and get cast on a sitcom or sell a script by then. But it's simply not going to happen. You can't count on money coming in for a script you haven't sold (or finished), or from a job you've interviewed for but haven't gotten. And yet Christians do this all the time, assuming that they're showing profound faith.

Assume you'll have to pay your way for six years instead of six months. Get the skills you need.

### *Joy in Living in Los Angeles*

I love L.A. (Me and Randy Newman.) Granted, it took a while. And it may take you a while. But if you never learn to like living in a place so spread out that your best friend could live fifteen miles away, your job twenty miles away, your church twenty-five miles away, and your writing group thirty miles away—all in different directions . . . well, why would you spend your life being homesick?

I have an old college friend from England who likes to say, "L.A. is a great place to live, but I wouldn't want to visit there." And I think he's right. It's a tough place to get used to for many, but one day you find yourself defending it, and you realize, *I wouldn't want to live anywhere else.*

I can hear you thinking now, *But I'm a writer. A writer can write from anywhere! I don't have to live in L.A.* Um, sorry, but yes, you do. Our agent likes to say, "You can have a screen-writing career outside of L.A., but you can't start a screenwriting career outside of L.A." You're going to have to make the move, but hopefully you'll love it.

### *A Life outside the Industry*

Your life must be more than your career. Sure, you need technical knowledge of your craft and a working understanding of how the biz works. But you need so much more!

You need balance. You need church, friends, exercise, relaxation, inspirational input. You need a life! Make sure you keep what you've got, and don't let it be sucked up by the all-demanding industry.

## So . . . Should You Come to Hollywood?

Iconoclast Hunter S. Thompson once described television journalism as a "cruel and shallow money trench . . . a long plastic hallway where thieves and pimps run free and good men die like dogs."[3] He could just as well have been describing the movie business—or Hollywood in general.

Have I scared you off yet? If I have, maybe I've done you the biggest favor of your life. But if you've read this far, if you've weighed your motives and found them healthy, if you're talented, if you're ambitious, if you're dedicated and persevering, if you're wise, if you want to learn and grow and contribute and serve . . .

Then—please—come to Hollywood. And welcome!

---

**Notes**

1. 2003 L. A. Screenwriting Expo.
2. "My Hope Is Built on Nothing Less," lyrics by Edward Mote (1834), music by William B. Bradbury (1836).
3. Hunter S. Thompson, *Generation of Swine: Tales of Shame and Degradation in the '80s* (New York: Summit Books, 1988).

# 9  A Hollywood Survival Guide

## Ralph Winter

The key to surviving in Hollywood is to think of your time here as a journey similar to the journey of a hero in a screenplay. Every great screen hero, in order to obtain the object of his quest, must first go through the desert of the second act. If you're trying to make it in the entertainment industry, you will face many deserts: rejection, lack of focus, isolation. For Christians, the terrain is even more treacherous. You will face temptations, challenges, perhaps even prejudice.

Many people trying to break into the entertainment business, in their eagerness, rush right in without considering the challenges they will face. No time to waste, right? Wrong.

Ralph Winter has produced a string of mega-blockbusters, including *X-Men*; *X2: X-Men United*; *Fantastic Four*; *I, Robot*; *Planet of the Apes*; *Star Trek IV: The Voyage Home*; and the upcoming *X-Men 3*. Beginning his career making training videos for a department store, Winter moved on to do post-production work on television shows such as *Happy Days, Laverne and Shirley, Taxi*, and *Mork and Mindy*. He started as a producer on *Star Trek III: The Search for Spock*. He is a member of the Directors Guild of America and the Academy of Motion Picture Arts and Sciences. He is also a juror for the Angelus Awards and the Damah Film Festival.

With this attitude, you will find yourself stranded in the desert without water or a compass. The hero always considers the journey ahead, the deserts that may lie before him, and prepares accordingly.

Having been on this journey for some years now, and having survived the desert, I can give you some idea of what you'll face and what you can do to survive.

## Preserving Your Relationships

The entertainment business is not friendly to families and relationships. I got married before I ever thought of becoming involved in the movie world. And though Judy and I have been happily married for over thirty years, it's not been without its rough spots. In this industry, being married is a choice we have to make every day.

After producing several of the *Star Trek* movies, I was eager to broaden my career. I got an offer to produce the movie *Captain Ron* at Disney. It was a great opportunity. Being the sole producer for a large project and having international experience are crucial to building your professional reputation.

The shoot would require me to spend six months in Puerto Rico. My family was young. I had a thirteen-year-old daughter and an eighteen-year-old son. But they knew it would be hard while I was building a career. We had all signed on, so to speak. I took the job. Once a month I either flew the family down to Puerto Rico or I went home for the weekend. Sometimes I would just fly my wife in for a few days. We worked it out.

Two years later, I had another terrific opportunity. I was taking the rare vacation with my family when I got an offer to take over a movie shooting in New York and London. Before I knew it, I was in London meeting with the director and the crew.

Preproduction went well, and I soon became accustomed to hopping back and forth between New York and London. Four weeks in, I flew the kids out for a long weekend. We were watching the Broadway production of *Beauty and the Beast* when I got an urgent page from my wife. Something terrible had happened. Her father had died in tragic circumstances.

We arranged for the kids to return home. Friends and family rallied around my wife while I flew to London for the first days of photography. Being fairly new on the job, I felt that I had to be there. As producer, I was responsible for making sure everything went smoothly.

Thanks to our pastor and close friends, my wife was surrounded by support. And I spent every spare minute I had on the phone with her from New York or London. While we struggled through those weeks, the production went well. It went so well, in fact, that the studio asked me to move immediately to another project once we wrapped, a James Bond movie.

I have always been partial to the Bond movies, and the thought of adding the credit to my resume was exhilarating. I knew I would have to discuss it with my wife, so I told the studio I needed time to decide. I flew Judy to New York and brought her flowers and champagne from London. We stayed at the Ritz, and we walked around New York, talking about the opportunity.

Even as I write this, I cannot believe how selfish I was, how unfeeling I was about her ongoing grief and depression. I was caught up in the excitement of Hollywood and the possibilities of my own career. God spoke through her that weekend as she clearly laid out what steps would have to be taken for our relationship and our future. I could not spend another six months out of the country at such a crucial time in our family. I returned to London and told the studio head I was turning down the opportunity. I will never forget his response.

"So the job is too tough?"

"No," I said. "I can't spend that kind of time away from my family right now."

He couldn't understand what I was saying. In his mind nothing could be worth turning down a Bond film. That was our last conversation. I never worked for that studio again.

The London movie turned out well, but when I went looking for my next project, nothing was available. I sat at home, draining my bank accounts and my savings. I prayed that something would come my way. After some months, I began to get angry with God. "I made this decision to turn down a movie. I did what you told me was the right thing, and now I am unemployed?"

After six months without work, I got a call from a friend. He asked if I wanted to work on a television series that would shoot in the San Fernando Valley—not far from where we lived. And the series was being executive produced by a guy named Steven Spielberg. Suddenly, God's plan became clear.

Working with Steven energized my career like no Bond movie ever could. I don't look for God to answer all my prayers in this way. But I do understand now that while projects come and go, families do not. And if you can remember that while working here in Hollywood, your family will be there when all the movies are over.

My wife has been instrumental in reminding me that family is a priority. And I am very blessed that she has been so understanding about the nature of this business. She put up with all the hours I had to spend away from the family early in my career, when I was still paying my dues. One year while I was at Paramount, I was asked to attend a meeting at a producer's home on Easter Sunday. Judy reluctantly took the kids to church without me.

She has realized that I will never be home for dinner at 5:30 p.m. In Hollywood, 5:30 is when things are just getting started. When we were remodeling our home, we stayed with her parents. They asked her nearly every day if I would be home for dinner by 6:00 p.m. They couldn't understand what kind of job would keep you any later.

Being a producer is entrepreneurial, and like other self-starting businesses (e.g., real estate), there are no "work hours." The job never stops. There are always phone calls to take, meetings and screenings to attend, scripts to read, etc. To survive, you have to be discerning. Is that screening really so important? Can I afford to miss that meeting? In this business, time is precious. But I've learned that time with my family is even more precious. And so I let the phone ring during dinner; I commit to time with my family; and I check in with my wife at least once during the day.

Relationships are key to success in Hollywood. For a Christian, they are also integral to maintaining a godly and balanced life. As with any achievement in this business, holy and grounding relationships will not happen accidentally. They must be sought, nourished, and continually deepened.

### Maintaining Your Sanity

The entertainment business is hard on relationships, but it's just as hard on your own spiritual well-being. It's easy to lose focus, to forget your priorities and wander from the path. There is not any one thing you can do to survive this desert. It's a matter of maintenance, of the small things you do every day and every week to keep the engine running smoothly.

Judy and I have been part of a small weekly Bible study for years. With the constant demands of movie production, this is no small feat, but we make it a priority. The benefit, short of less therapy time, is that we have a community of faith that cares about us and whom we can rely on. It sustains us through all the weird stuff that goes on in Hollywood. And the refreshing part is that this is a group of non-industry Christians. They don't care about the movie business; they treat me like everyone else in the group. The fact that this is so rare in Hollywood makes it all the more valuable to us.

For the past ten years, I have also met weekly with two men. These guys are not in the movie business, but they are very successful in the insurance business and broadcast business. We challenge each other about how we spend our time, how we spend our money, and if we are doing enough to give of ourselves as Christ gave to us. One of them sponsors houseboat trips for inner-city kids at a lake in northern California. The other is the chairman of Special Olympics and the parent of a child with disabilities.

Finally, I attend church regularly and remain active there. If you don't get plugged in at a church and have some kind of support group for your personal growth, you will have nothing to give in your work. And, if you lose your job, you will have nothing to fall back on. If you are out there pitching yourself as an actor and getting rejected, who will tell you that you are worthwhile?

Maintaining your sanity in Hollywood means keeping a routine of regular commitments that keep you focused on what really matters and challenge you to be a better person.

### Striking a Balance

Christians are always asking how I maintain my faith while working in Hollywood. My usual smart-aleck response is that it is no harder to balance your life in Hollywood than it is in Silicon Valley or on Wall Street. In any of these places, you can become consumed with what is immediately before your eyes—making the deal, finishing the project, selling the product. In any of these places, you can become distracted by the pursuit of purely wordly goals, forgetting your call to be salt and light in the world and heralds of God's coming kingdom.

But to answer the question, I maintain my faith in Hollywood by always trying to love and serve through my work. Wherever we are, we can learn to balance our ambitions with our higher duties. And, I believe, this is the only way to demonstrate in the workplace how we are being changed as followers of Christ.

I work hard at my craft to bring the best stories to the screen. But Christ taught us that it matters how we treat people and how we act while pursuing that call. With all my staff and crew, I take the attitude "How can I help *you* do *your* job?" I have found that this is not only the best way for me to serve them, but it also just plain works. If I did their job for them, I would demean them. But when I affirm and support them, they do the job better than I ever could have. And as an added benefit, when my team does well, it reflects well on me.

In my years in the industry, an offer to pray for a co-worker or employee has never been turned down. Sometimes I am the only one to go and pray with that person from the crew. And it is so significant to them that often, after not seeing me for years, they will come up to me and remind me of how I came to them in the name of Christ.

I also choose to serve my bosses at the studio. Yes, they sign my paychecks, but that doesn't mean I can't still serve them—by making their jobs easier and not complaining when they make mine harder.

### You're Not Alone

No matter what desert you are traveling through, be it a Hollywood career or some other challenge, remember that God is with you at every step. He is your constant companion on the journey. And he is the only one you can always count on to be there.

The most important thing I've learned from my own journey is this: the best thing you can do to prepare for the road ahead is to deepen your personal relationship with Christ. If you can do that, you'll find him waiting for you at the other end of the desert, in the third act of your life.

# 10        Toward a
# Christian Cinema

## Barbara Nicolosi

"I want to be the next Mel Gibson!" With flashing eyes and
buoyed on by the nods of his friends, twentysomething Jeremy
radiated the zealous conviction of a seventh-century crusader
preparing to take back the Holy Land. His was a sentiment
I have encountered innumerable times in Christian settings
since the spring of 2004. Mel Gibson's *The Passion of the Christ*
went off like a lightbulb in the collective consciousness of
the Christian church, awakening everyone to the power in
cinema to spread the Good News. At this particular moment
I was giving a talk at a Christian college, and young Jeremy

Barbara Nicolosi is executive director of Act One. She has an MA in film from
Northwestern University in Evanston, Illinois. She has been a director of development,
a panelist for the National Endowment for the Arts, and a consultant on many film and
television projects. She wrote *The Work*, a full-length feature set during the Spanish Civil
War, for IMMI Pictures of Beverly Hills. Her feature screenplay *Select Society* is being
developed by Reel Life Women Productions, Bel Air. She writes a media column for the
*National Catholic Register*, is on the executive committee of the City of the Angels Film
Festival, and is on the board of Catholics in Media. She frequently addresses writers
conferences on screenwriting and the arts.

had sprung to his feet as soon as the question period began. He followed up with, "Tell me what I need to do to make the next *Passion of the Christ*."

I suddenly had a whole new insight into the Gospel passage between Jesus and the rich young man. I think I kept the sigh out of my voice. "Give away everything that you have and are now doing so that you can throw yourself into mastering the cinematic art form. Get your act together spiritually, and then do everything you can to get into a top film school. Study philosophy and theology so that you have something real to say through your movies. Read lots of classic novels and write hundreds of pages so that you achieve command of the language as a creative tool. Get your moral act together so that you won't get tripped up too easily in the whirl of the entertainment business. Then, come and follow us by moving to Los Angeles. And in ten or fifteen years, maybe you'll see your name on the screen appended to a movie of lasting value."

Needless to say, like the young man in the Gospel, Jeremy's face fell, and he too went away sad.

*The Passion of the Christ* did not come out of nowhere. It came thirty years into Mel Gibson's filmmaking experience mainly at the top levels of the industry. It came almost a decade after he produced his Oscar-winning film, *Braveheart*. It came fifteen years after his profound conversion and the reorienting of his life to Christ. The film itself took ten years of a brooding, devastating, creative journey. Many people in the church have been asking me if, in the wake of *The Passion*'s success, Hollywood will produce many more such movies. "Hollywood" can't! There will be no other *Passions* without other Mel Gibsons to bring them into being.

As a talented filmmaker who is a devout Christian, Mel Gibson is absolutely an anomaly in Hollywood at the dawn of the twenty-first century. The reason for this comes down to the fact that artists who have talent and mastery of the craft very rarely believe in Christ, and that Christians who have any kind of mature faith very rarely have the passion, perseverance, and professionalism to succeed in the entertainment business.

It's not that Christians aren't making stabs at moviemaking and television production. It's that most of these efforts come to naught because our fears and misconceptions have us standing on the sidelines, cursing and boycotting and begging for favors from the pagans who have paid their dues and have the power to green-light stories for the screen. The whole church needs to brood over what it means to be the Patron of the Arts in a post-Christian setting. We need to wrangle over how best to nurture our young artists and media professionals, and how to maximize the influence of those Christians with talent and charisma. But first of all, we need to figure out what success in Hollywood will look like for the Christian community. What does a Christian worldview mean in entertainment, and will our own brothers and sisters in the church recognize it when our artists start producing it?

## People, Not Projects

Several years ago, I was approached by a group of Christians from somewhere back East who had decided that it was time for Christians to make "our kind of movies." They had collected nearly a million dollars from some concerned Christian millionaires, and they were ready to make a biopic of a Catholic saint that would "show Hollywood." They wanted me to read their screenplay, I suppose, for affirmation. It quickly became obvious that they didn't really want any advice.

The script was awful. None of the folks involved in the production had ever made a movie before. The producer was also to be the co-writer, director, and one of the stars in the film. He had never directed a movie before, nor had he or his co-writer ever written a movie before. They had no stars in their cast, no studio attached to help finance and distribute the film, and no money left over for marketing. When I presented all of these as problems, they responded with gentle laughter and said, "Barb, God is going to make this movie great."

Well, the movie came out to a chorus of "mediocres" from both secular and religious critics. One major secular critic asked of the film's main character, "Why was this woman even a saint?" The impact of such projects on the perception of Christianity in Hollywood can only be described as devastating. Substandard work makes us look unprofessional, ignorant, lacking in respect, and fundamentally deficient in depth and intelligence. In this case, the film failed to secure theatrical distribution, of course, and so will ultimately go down in the books as a million-dollar waste of time and resources. And in the ultimate irony, not only did the project not convert Hollywood, its failure left many of its coalition of volunteers and investors pointing fingers of blame, alienated from each other and in denial.

Sadly, I have seen this same story played out at least ten times in the last few years. It reflects one of the most crippling misconceptions that the Christian community has to flush out of its system before we will make any kind of coordinated beachhead in the entertainment industry. When we speak of achieving a "Christian cinema," we don't mean a creative ghetto for us to come together and make product all by ourselves and for ourselves. God is not at all invested in the church "showing Hollywood" with isolated and mediocre projects. He is invested in the *people* here, in the hearts and minds of those whom he has touched with artistic talent, who in this strange moment of human history have wandered far from him. Our efforts to make films and television in a "safe" Christian envelope will not be blessed. We need to be in the middle of the industry, on the lots, on the sets, and in the network and studio offices, working side by side with those who do not share our worldview, so as to bring God where he is not.

We need to humbly acknowledge as a Christian community that we do not have "masters" of the screen art form in our midst. We should be driven to work with the pagans not just to bring Christ to them but also, frankly, to learn from them. Many believers disdain learning from Hollywood people, because they have a sense of moral superiority. The fact is, just because someone doesn't worship Jesus does not mean they have nothing to offer when it comes to creating compelling characters. I have had many believers sniff to me that they don't want to work in Hollywood because they don't want to be polluted by the industry's moral climate. But Christians stay away just as often, because we don't want to be embarrassed by the fact that the secular professionals are so much better than we are at making art.

Finally, our efforts in entertainment cannot be limited to making movies about saints and the Bible, as though we have nothing to say to the modern world about anything that is not part of our subculture. Borrowing from St. Paul, Christians in entertainment don't have to be always talking about God. They should be talking about everything in a godly way.

If the church is going to make headway in cinema and television, we need to know what it is we are talking about when we refer to the screen art forms. What are the limits and possibilities of the screen as a means of expression? What are the realities that define these art forms? A lot of us will not embrace the entertainment world because there are things about it that fundamentally rub us the wrong way as Christians. Are these things really dangerous, or are we ourselves the problem here?

### *A Visual Medium*

I constantly hear believers speak in dark, ominous tones about the fact that this culture is becoming "increasingly more visual." We are people of the Word, and so we are uncomfortable in abandoning our verbal formulations for the imprecise communication of imagery. But in no way are words superior to images as a means of communication. The two are just different.

Images absolutely can convey truth. Indeed, they convey a much broader and more universal kind of information than any message framed in words. Unmediated by language, a picture connects viscerally to the memory and delivers its meaning directly to the understanding. The message conveyed through an image can't be defined in words. If it could, we wouldn't be driven as artists to create the image. The images that flash by in a movie combine uniquely with every individual's experience to form a slightly different message in everyone. This is true in verbal communication too. We cannot ensure what our audience actually hears in what we say. But at least we can know what we have said. When we use images, we tend to say much more than we can even express ourselves.

It is worth noting that cinema is much more than "a visual medium." Saying cinema is a visual medium is like saying Van Gogh was a painter who worked in yellow. He did, of course, along with every other color in the spectrum. If art is selection and beauty is harmonious selection, a beautiful movie is a harmony of harmonies. A work of cinema includes literature (screenwriting); painting (composition); acting; architecture and sculpture (set design); hair, makeup, and costume design; sound design; photography; musical composition; and computer-generated effects. It is difficult to come up with an art form that isn't a part of cinema.

But minimally, movies and television are visual in three ways: imagery, composition, and the juxtaposition of images. Christian filmmakers will not be able to represent our vision of the world until we become masters of poetic imagery. We need to learn how to place and light objects in a frame so as to form pictures that will haunt our viewers in a saving way. We need to learn how to edit together disparate images to lead the viewers to make new and more profound associations and connections.

The things we Christians want to say to the world are the big, universal, "beyond mere language" kind. Whenever we make a movie that delivers its message principally in dialogue, it feels sickeningly simple and insulting to the audience. We should not be uncomfortable with the visual aspect of cinema. Far from it. It can be the salvation of the message we bear.

### A Collaborative Medium

Once at a conference of Christian scholars, I was approached by a philosopher who took issue with my use of the word *art* to refer to cinema. "I don't believe in art by committee," he said. He spoke for many believers who see the corporate, collaborative climate that drives Hollywood productions as being incompatible with the sacred solitude that beauty demands.

This is a false dichotomy. As noted earlier, the screen art forms are a composite kind of art. Cinema is the harmonious marriage of the creative processes of scores of different kinds of artists into one whole. In the entertainment industry, a cinema or television project is said to "work" when a vision has been well communicated to a large group, and their contributions complement the initial vision, making the whole project an effective unity. The fundamental "sacred" vision is not lost in the collaborative process but expanded.

### Perpetually Modern

Too many Christians have adopted the view that anything new is unnecessary or even bad. I'll never forget the preacher I met at a conference who waved his Bible at me and said,

"These are the only stories anyone ever needs." He was actually betraying himself as someone who is afraid that the Bible can't compete with secular storytelling. The Bible has nothing to fear from literature!

The screen art forms are modern in a philosophical sense as well as in a technological sense. Primarily developed in the twentieth century, cinema has existed only in the period after modern philosophy proclaimed "God is dead." All the confusions of this past century have been the subject of the art form. There isn't a Renaissance cinema that could balance out the artistic confusion of the last hundred years the way Michelangelo balances out Andy Warhol and thus keeps painting as a fine art in the minds of contemporary Christians.

Christianity has been the primary victim of modernism. We were on the defensive most of the twentieth century, defending our institutions, rituals, and structures, specifically against the charge that we are anti-progressive. This charge has been played out on the screen time and time again, and especially since the sexual revolution, the ideological offspring of modernism. We just haven't seen our ideas played out on the screen with the power and depth with which they have been attacked on the screen. So, our people see the screen as the enemy and are cynical about adopting it.

### Linked to Technology

Again, because of our sense that creativity should have a kind of sacredness to it, Christians are sometimes put off by all the machines that mediate the art forms of screen and television. The production process just seems too big to have any holy intimacy about it. How can it be the work of an artist's hands if it is coming from something you have to plug in? We tend to be very suspicious that the fruit of the screen is really coming from a machine, instead of from a person.

In truth, we don't even know what to call the screen art form because it keeps changing. The thing that viewers have enjoyed in darkened theaters for the last hundred years has gone from being "moving pictures" to "picture shows" in the early days of the nickelodeon to "silent films" to "talkies" to "movies." Each of these periods has had its own masters and classics. Virginia Woolf complained in the early thirties that "the problem with cinema is that its technology is perpetually outgrowing its aesthetic accomplishments." It would be as though every five years, ten new colors were discovered that painters could then use on their canvases.

The fact that cinema is tied to technology does not diminish its stature as an art form. It just makes it more difficult to follow the development of the art form. Pope John Paul II noted that the very fact that cinema comes from technology is a sign that it is a gift of God to the modern age. He pointed out that it is technology that has fragmented the human family, and so it is appropriate that God would send a means of technology to create a new kind of communion between us.

### Show "Business"

As art forms, cinema and television are much like architecture in that the palette and canvas of the artist represents a huge investment. A 2004 article in the industry trades noted that due to the advances in digital editing technology, the average cost of making a movie has fallen "way down" in recent years to just around twenty-six million dollars. Because movies are so expensive to produce, there is always a commercial aspect involved in shaping them. Again, believers tend to see the corporate presence in the industry as defiling the creative process.

The truth is, as many times as an industry executive messes up a great movie to generate more sales, somewhere else an executive encourages a change that will make a project more accessible, more engaging, and more compelling. I have experienced the commercial aspect of the business as one of the best checks on the quality of the ultimate product. If you have to sell something, it has to have something of the beautiful or at least the well crafted to attract buyers.

### It's about the Questions

A very successful television writer once told me the secret of her career. She said, "In every show, I never try and solve problems. I just try and frame one important question."

The reason that so many screen projects from Christians fail is because they fail to respect the appropriate role of art. Art has a "prophetic role" in the sense of calling us beyond the mundane to brood and ponder and think as only we, among all creation, can do. It violates the purpose of art when the makers try to do the thinking for the viewers. I have found that Christians who have money to invest in movies tend to be particularly demanding that they see a "dollar for dollar" return in the screenplay. The "dollar" they want to see on the screen is the overt articulation of theological truth. Ironically, projects like this actually turn off the audience for whom they are intended. It is a subversion of the medium to try and force it to achieve something beyond its possibility.

Entertainment is best when it poses compelling questions, when it is not a lesson for the viewer but a dialogue with the viewer. A movie can show the ramifications of a worldview, but it gets in real trouble when it starts articulating worldviews. Christians will never have real success in Hollywood until we accept that simply delivering the Truth will not help the audience. We must allow the audience to wrestle with the Truth.

We need to have the simple trust of the sower who casts seeds out on the ground and then moves on, believing that somebody else will come along to till, weed, and harvest.

Why is it that people of faith have so little faith in people?

### *It's Just Entertainment*

There is a perpetual tension in Hollywood between the projects that are meant to serve the audience and those that are meant to serve as personal expression for the filmmaker. This tension is magnified in the church, which questions if marrying its prophetic message to mere entertainment isn't somehow sacrilegious. Many Christians do not appreciate entertainment in the sense in which philosopher Josef Pieper called "Leisure, the basis of culture." Some would argue that worship or work is the basis of culture. As one haughty deacon expressed it to me once, "The church is in the business of saving, not entertaining." I responded to him, "And do you think the disciples found Jesus boring?"

We Christians could bring much to this industry by simply elevating our view of entertainment to the idea that it is fundamentally an act of charity and service to the audience. I once spoke to a television sitcom writer, asking him what he felt was the lasting impact of his work on his viewers. He looked at me in confusion and, literally, scratched his head. "In twelve years of writing for television, it never occurred to me to do anything except keep the viewer from turning the channel." His goal has only ever been to amuse people in the sense of filling up their time, distracting them, but with no view to giving them anything helpful in living their lives. A Christian at the creative table would bear the needs of the global audience in his heart. He would instinctively gravitate toward projects that would be truly re-creative for viewers,

125

projects that provide moments of awe and transcendence, moments of self-discovery, and moments of deeper connection with other people.

## The Goal

So, what is a Christian movie? Many godly people think that the goal is for movies to be "non-offensive" in terms of sex, language, and violence. But the problem with that standard is it only describes a void. It doesn't give any creative guidance. A lot of Christians lauded the 2002 release *A Walk to Remember* mainly on this basis: "It didn't have any bad language, and the two teenagers didn't sleep together." Yes, but it was a banal, predictable story with underdeveloped characters, pedestrian acting, and saccharine dialogue.

There aren't going to be any simple narrative guidelines that make a project acceptable. Sometimes, it will serve the Truth to have the bad guys get away with murder, as in the 2002 film *In the Bedroom.* This project, which dealt with the spiritual and psychological urgency of forgiveness, was rejected by many Christians because the film's two protagonists kill someone in revenge and don't get caught. "Yes," I groaned to one indignant pastor, "but the characters are insane at the end of the film! No one wants to be them!" He responded, "I just think it would have been better if they had ended up in jail." Ironically, the film is more haunting because the two characters don't end up in a man-made jail but in a psychological prison of their own making.

While Christian projects will not be defined by the topics they treat, we can expect that certain defining themes will inhere in our projects as the cinematic "aroma of Christ." Beyond just good human values, which Hollywood can manufacture on most days without us, Christians need to be in the entertainment industry to bring to the fore our defining values.

So what would be some of the themes that would define a Christian movie?

### Affirmation of Spiritual Realities

The twentieth-century Christian apologist Frank Sheed distinguished Christian storytellers from pagan ones by the fact that Christian writers live in a world that is as much driven by spiritual realities as by material ones. He noted, "The secular novelist sees what is visible; the Christian novelist sees what is there."

Created with a Christian sensibility, a movie should be haunted by the invisible world. For believers, everything that we see is a sign of a reality that we cannot see. Paraphrasing St. Paul, all of creation points to the Presence and Nature of the Creator. Or, as Jesuit writer William Lynch has noted, "Faith is the ability of the finite to lead somewhere." A movie made with this conviction will leave viewers with the sense that beyond all the chaos and craziness in the world is a Loving Mind that comprehends it all, and is over it all.

This broader vision—encompassing what is seen with the heart as well as with the eyes—has as much to do with good writing as with pastoral urgency. As writer Flannery O'Connor expressed it, "The real novelist, the one with an instinct for what he is about, knows that he cannot approach the infinite directly. He must penetrate the natural human world as it is. The more sacramental his theology, the more encouragement he will get from it to do just that."[1]

### Connectedness

A Christian film should be imbued with the certainty that we are not alone. We were conceived of, worked out, prepared for, and assigned a place in the plan. We are connected to one another and to the One who yearns for us as the apple of his eye. Humans are meant to be merciful to one another. Talents are given to us to speed us corporately on our way home to God. We should treat human beings the way we would treat any unique and precious treasure that belongs to someone else.

### Good and Evil Are Not Equal

Despite how it seems to a merely human perspective, good and evil are not locked in an equal struggle. The good is much greater, because it can incorporate every evil and turn it into a good.

A Christian dramatist needs to portray sin with the same intensity as does a purely secular dramatist because, as Flannery O'Connor noted, "Redemption is meaningless unless there is a cause for it in the actual life we live."[2] But a Christian movie would ultimately lead viewers away from cynicism and toward hope. As Auschwitz survivor Corrie ten Boom expressed it, "We know that there is no pit so deep, that God's love isn't deeper still."[3]

### The Culture of Life

Coined by Pope John Paul II, the term "the culture of life" encapsulates the attitude toward human persons that defines Christians. Pope John Paul II distinguishes the reverence with which believers approach the human person from what he calls secularism's "culture of death." A society has bought into the culture of death, the pope notes, whenever it concludes that the resolution to a social problem can be found in the death of a person or group of people.

A Christian project will emanate the certainty that men and women are the summit of everything created. If rareness makes something valuable, then human beings are precious in their uniqueness. Human beings are not valuable because of what they can do but because of what they are: vessels of love. Love called forth to be poured in. Love seeping out on those around. Humans are a unity of matter and spirit, making each person a mystery. As G. K. Chesterton expressed it, "The merely human is inhuman."[4] And so a Christian movie will reflect a reverence in its bearing toward the human person. There will be things a Christian movie can look at in human experience and other things from which it will turn its gaze in a sense of privacy.

Our reverence to persons will dictate not only the kinds of stories that we tell but also the method in which we tell them. We will not ask actors to violate themselves for our art, because Christians reject that a person can ever be used for any purpose—even for drama. Further, we can't manipulate, coerce, propagandize, or deceive.

### *Juxtaposition of Joy and Suffering*

When we first started Act One back in 1999, I was interviewed by Howard Rosenberg, the hard-bitten *Los Angeles Times* television reporter. Howard had been on the beat for decades and had a reputation for skewering Christians in his column. After asking me many questions about our hopes for our new program, Howard sighed and said, "Even if you people are wrong, we need you here because you bring a note of hope."

The weirdest thing about Christians is the way we can hold both terrible suffering and joy in our hands at the same time without any sense of contradiction. Good Friday is at once the worst thing that ever happened and the best thing that ever happened. In every death, we see the seeds of resurrections, and so our grief can never be complete, as in despair.

Because of this, our stories are always going to emit an aroma of hope. Comfortable with this mystery, as the human creature's lot in life, we do not have to resolve every conflict in our stories. But our unresolved conflicts will always reflect our conviction that, as screenwriter and novelist Karen Hall has said, "I may not understand the reason why, but I know Someone does."

### But Will It Sell?

The capacity for a product to sell: this is a primary paradox for Christian writers and producers in Hollywood. On the one hand, we have vital stories and themes that we want to see produced. We stress with our community of Act One writers that the first thing they need to have in starting to write is passion for the subject matter. A writer who isn't passionate about the material will not be able to weather all the sacrifices and obstacles the project will require.

On the other hand, professionalism demands that we offer a product that will be saleable. Too often writers who pitch me movie ideas will be stymied when I ask them the necessary question, "And why will people want to see this movie now? What will drive millions of people to the movie theaters to see this story?"

This doesn't have to be a paralyzing problem for Christians in Hollywood. The answer to the problem of commerciality is to find the intersection of our themes with the current cries of the world. What is it that the people of our world are worried about today? What are the most urgent fears of this generation? These are the "signs of the times" for the church in this age, and particularly for those of us who are storytellers.

Once we have identified the world's cries, we need to examine our own hearts to see which of our defining Christian themes most correspond. Pastoral entertainment doesn't tell people what we think they need to hear but rather listens first of all.

## To Reiterate: People, Not Projects

The principal reason for the moral confusion that ends up on the screen is the paucity of happy, well-catechized believers in the entertainment industry. We do not have enough witnesses to Christ living and loving and working alongside the witnesses to Mammon or secular humanism that have overrun the creative community. We do not have enough thoughtful, godly filmmakers who can draw compelling stories from a mature faith experience.

The world does not need a "Christian cinema" so much as it needs Christians in cinema.

We do not need our churches to set up production companies and make movies. We need the church to approach Hollywood as a missionary territory, to preach and teach and minister. We need a new generation of artist-apostles to come to the industry with humility and pastoral love.

**Notes**

1. Flannery O'Connor, *Mystery and Manners* (New York: Farrar, Straus, and Giroux, 1969).

2. Stephen Sparrow, "No Place Like Home," March 2002, www.mediaspecialist.org/ssnoplace.html.

3. Corrie ten Boom, *The Hiding Place* (New York: Bantam Books, 1974).

4. G. K. Chesterton, *The Everlasting Man* (San Francisco: Ignatius Press, 1993).

# 11 What Would Jesus Write?

## Sheryl Anderson

A great many people who meet me through the Christian writers community are taken aback by the fact that I worked on the first three seasons of *Charmed*, a television program about three sisters who are witches. I understand; it's not the first show that leaps to mind when you think about Christians working in Hollywood.

In fact, I hadn't been on the show more than a week or so when one of the executive producers knocked on my office door. He clearly wasn't happy, and I immediately tried to figure out what I had done, or failed to do, to earn his displeasure. But he was headed in a different direction altogether. "You go to church, right?" he snapped.

I had a bizarre moment of panic. *They found me out!* "Yes, why?" I answered.

Sheryl Anderson has been a television studio executive, a half-hour writer (*Parker Lewis Can't Lose*, *Dave's World*), and is now an hour writer/producer (*Charmed*, *For the People*). Sheryl also writes the Molly Forrester novels (*Killer Heels*, *Killer Cocktail*) with her husband, Mark Parrott.

133

"Come here." He disappeared from my doorway, leaving me to scramble down the hallway after him into his office. Had he decided we were going to have to work every Sunday, and he was anticipating a problem from me? Why else would my going to church bother him? I won't bore you with the litany of imagined offenses I raced through, trying to think what I could have possibly done to earn such a summons and what it had to do with my going to church.

When I caught up with him at his office, the other executive producer, the woman who created the show, was waiting for us. Together, they explained to me that one of the actresses who had appeared in the pilot episode of the show was having second thoughts about continuing with the series because of her spiritual beliefs.

On a purely practical level, this was a huge problem. We were about to start production for the first season. If she couldn't continue, we would have to recast and then reshoot large portions of the pilot. It was daunting to calculate the financial and logistical hit the show was about to take.

They wanted me to explain to her why it was all right for a practicing Christian to be on a show that dealt with magic and demons and witches.

I was willing to help. I was already enjoying the show, the people on it, the possibilities of it. But the producers unknowingly hit one of my sore spots when it comes to Christianity in Hollywood—the assumption that because all Christians share a common belief in Jesus Christ as our Savior, we all believe the same things.

I'm a member of a denomination whose various synods don't even agree on pivotal matters of doctrine. How could I assume what this actress's comfort level would be, just because she was also Christian? I couldn't. I told the executive producers that I'd be happy to talk to her, but that there was no guarantee I could convince her, because her beliefs might differ pretty wildly from mine.

I have to admit, I thought this would be an interesting opportunity to discuss all the justifications I had for being on the show with another believer and see what her reaction would be. I wondered if I'd be able to win her over to my way of thinking.

It would not be the first time I'd had a conversation along these lines. I'd already dealt with friends at church who didn't hide their disappointment with my decision when I first decided to take the job, whereas I actually thought the job was a fantastic opportunity. Here was a show about good versus evil, where good won every week. A show about the primacy and power of familial love. Most important, I saw it as a series about the challenge of being given talents by a greater power and struggling to find the most fulfilling way to use them. To me, it was a weekly morality play—even with the way some of the actresses preferred to dress.

I met with the actress. I wish I could say that I was able to persuade her, but I wasn't. We had a lengthy conversation, but she didn't change her mind. To this day, I don't know all the questions that rose up in her heart to keep her from continuing with the series, but they were strong enough that she had to leave. I had to respect that.

I also had to reexamine my decision to be on the show. Was I being shortsighted? Was I ignoring important spiritual issues in my eagerness to work? *Charmed* represented my transition from half-hour writing to hour writing, a change I'd been eager to make. Was I putting that desire higher than it should be? I prayed about it and felt reassured that I should stay even though I couldn't be sure exactly what I was meant to accomplish while I was there. (I've often said that in my personal version of "Footprints," when I look back over my shoulder, I don't see the one pair of footprints where Jesus carried me; I see the two trenches caused by my heels as he dragged me from where I was to where I needed to be.)

After the actress left the show, the part was recast, production resumed, and the show became successful in fairly short order. The first episode I wrote involved the three sisters meeting an ancestress who traveled through time to help them with a problem and, in so doing, taught them about their family history and the role they were destined to play. There was a great deal of talk about the importance of the family and their love for each other being key to their power.

Several weeks after the episode aired, I received a letter written by a viewer. My first fan letter! It was written by a young woman who had been estranged from her family, from her mother in particular. She was so moved by the episode that she reconnected with her mother and was writing to thank me for helping to heal their rift.

That's why I write. To touch people. To move people. To make them think and feel. And as I read that letter I thought, *This is why I was led here.* To understand that there is a way, even with the most unlikely of premises, to communicate what I hold dear. To tell a story. Maybe not "the Story," but a story that could still contain the fruit of the Spirit.

Before going much farther, I should say that I don't normally think of myself as a Christian writer. I guess this is where I paraphrase the complaint of minority artists; I'm a writer who happens to be Christian. And a woman. And a wife, mother, mystery novelist, military brat, Redskins fan ... I love the Lord with my whole heart, but there are other factors, other concerns I bring to the table as well. There is a wide range of stories I want to tell. But I always search for a way to let my faith show through, no matter what I'm writing.

My husband and I write chancel dramas for the youth group at our church; we believe the talents God has given us should be used in his service, and we enjoy giving back to the church in this way. Plus, the kids get a kick out of it. We've also written the book for the middle school Christmas program the past two years. Last year, a middle school parent was praising the quality of the script, and a mutual friend introduced me as one of the authors. "It was so good. You should try and do something professionally," she enthused.

I smiled politely and explained that I was, in fact, a professional writer—a television writer, to be exact, even though I was not currently on a show. "Between projects" is the preferred euphemism.

She nodded enthusiastically. "You should go be on *Joan of Arcadia*. They could use you. Have you talked to them?"

I kept my polite smile, enjoying her vision of the television industry as one in which I could approach a show runner and say, "This is the show I want to be on. Where's my office?" But I also realized that my new friend was assuming that there were so few Christian writers in television that the only blatantly God-focused show on network television would still be in search of enough writers of faith to fill its ranks.

Certainly the majority of television programs on the air today do not announce themselves as programs written by people of faith. But both audience members and writers themselves have to look deeper and find the opportunities to celebrate faith that are a little more obscure, a little more subliminal. Exercises in what I like to call "stealth theology." Theology that gets to people in unexpected ways, that surprises them, that sneaks up on them while they think they're simply entertaining themselves.

Every program on television can't be *Joan of Arcadia*. Not even the most devout among us really want shows in which characters speak directly to God to fill every available hour of prime-time programming. We need diversity in entertainment. We need different points of view to challenge and excite us. God doesn't have to star in every show. But he can be in every show. Because he can be in every story we tell, even if he's just between the lines.

At one of the first Act One programs I attended, I was on a faculty panel of television writers. The moderator asked each of the students to name their favorite television show of all time and their favorite television show currently on the air. The panel members had to answer too, and when the question came to me, for my favorite show then on the air, I named *Oz*, Tom Fontana's brilliant and searing prison drama for HBO.

The participants were uniformly stunned, and some of my fellow panelists didn't look too pleased either. But I explained: yes, it was a program that dealt with brutality and inhumanity of the worst kind. But in doing so, it became a parable about redemption—about how our decision to accept or reject redemption defines every moment that follows. About how the possibility of redemption doesn't go away, no matter how far we fall. About what awaits us if we turn away. I was fascinated and pleased to see those questions being treated honestly and intelligently on television.

To think in programming terms, the Great Commission urges us to get out there and broaden our audience. Attract more viewers. Expand our demographic base. How do you do that? Tell them a great story.

The pastor of our church is a marvelous preacher. He has an "old school" style like Oswald Hoffman—a rich, powerful voice that can lilt with humor and then thunder with import. His sermons, which I adore, are anecdote driven; he likes to tell a series of stories to illustrate his point.

One morning, he began his sermon by admitting that a parishioner had come to him and complained that he told too many stories in his sermons.

"Jesus taught by telling stories, and it worked just fine for him. What better example can I follow?" he responded, and the number of anecdotes in his sermon hasn't diminished in the least.

The statement had a profound impact on me. I sat there in the sanctuary, thinking about Jesus as a storyteller. He knew the audience he was trying to reach, he'd defined his demographics, and he tailored his stories accordingly. He took complex theological concepts and turned them into clear, entertaining stories that even a child could understand. And the way he handled special effects! He'd do great in Hollywood today.

Most important, he didn't tell the same story over and over again. The theme may have been the same, but the story changed depending on his audience. He knew how to tailor his story to reach an audience that had to be challenged (the sower and his seeds), comforted (the Beatitudes), or shocked (the rich man and Lazarus).

If I'm striving to follow Jesus's example in all things, I thought, couldn't I follow it in this regard as well? Couldn't I learn to adapt the gospel no matter what shape my opportunity to share it took? Even if I wasn't on the staff of a show where faith was a natural subject, couldn't I fashion stories that served as parables on some level? If Jesus were sitting in front of this computer today, what would he write?

I started looking for opportunities in my scripts to talk about grace. Compassion. Forgiveness. And I was pleasantly surprised by how many opportunities there were. Because the key issues we struggle with as Christians are the key struggles of any human being—love, power, loss, meaning. Our victory as believers rises from our knowledge that there is meaning in the struggle. There is grace after the fight. But that's a message that can be conveyed in many ways, through many different stories. God doesn't have to be talking on the screen to speak through the story.

We can't confine our efforts or our support to programming that is explicitly Christian. We also need to produce and encourage programming that carries the seeds of faith implicitly and, by virtue of its more subtle demeanor, plants those seeds in hearts that might otherwise reject them. People will tune out a sermon because they don't want to (or feel they don't need to) be preached to. But no one can resist a well-crafted story.

If we want Christ to be seen everywhere, we have to be willing to see him everywhere, to look for his message everywhere. We have to be willing to write and to watch stories of redemption, charity, and love and celebrate the Spirit inherent in them. A television show doesn't need to have an angel in the cast to be about mercy. A film doesn't have to quote Scripture to put the gospel in people's hearts. If the world will know us by our fruits, then by our cop shows and romantic comedies and thrillers they can know us too.

I want to write so that the Good News is so entwined in the muscle of what I am writing that it can't be stripped away, can't be disregarded. We all know too many people who take their faith off and on like a favorite jacket—only wearing it when the weather gets cold or wet. The jacket, the armor of the gospel, is supposed to go on and stay on. It should be so intrinsic in our work that no matter what we write—overt gospel message, fanciful comedy, or procedural crime drama—the evidence of the Good News is there. I want to write the way I strive to live—completely integrated, so the Christian flows into the mother is bound to the wife is enmeshed with the friend. So you can't tell where my faith begins and stops because it doesn't. Because it is continuous and eternal, just like the love that inspires it.

I came to Hollywood because God gave me the gift of storytelling and I wanted to use it as fully as possible. I hope and I pray that no matter what kind of story I am telling, the light of my faith shines through, informs the story, and reaches the hearts of those who want and need to hear the message. I also hope and pray that the audience—whether they are people of faith or people in need of faith—will listen not just to the lines, but between the lines, to hear the story in a whole new way.

# 12 An Open Letter to Beginning Screenwriters

### Barbara Hall

Dear Screenwriters,

During the Vietnam conflict, Mother Teresa was asked by several protest groups if she would publicly speak out and join a march against the war. She said, "Absolutely not. But I will join any march you have for peace." St. Augustine said, "Love, and do what you will." Buddhists, too, believe in the importance of doing what you will, not what you must. And Jesus certainly had more dos than don'ts in his library of parables.

Barbara Hall was executive producer of *Joan of Arcadia*. Her producing credits include *Judging Amy, Chicago Hope, Northern Exposure, I'll Fly Away, Moonlighting*, and *Anything but Love*. She also developed three produced pilots and worked as story editor on *A Year in the Life* and *Newhart*. She wrote the feature films *Sylvie* and *Hearts*, in addition to authoring seven published novels. Barbara has garnered a Humanitas Award, Viewers for Quality Television, NAACP Image Award, TV Critics Association Award, American Library Association Best Books & Notable Books, four Emmy nominations, as well as a nomination for both the Writers Guild Award and the Producers Guild Award.

When asked to narrow the whole thing down to a digestible sound bite, what he came up with was this: "Love God with everything you've got. And while you're at it, love people." He told us how to approach life, not how to avoid it.

I make this point because in addressing you as beginning screenwriters, I want to encourage you to focus much more on possibilities than on restrictions or liabilities. Creative "dos" rather than "don'ts." I have no interest in discussing what you or anyone should leave out of their writing. I am interested in discussing what you can bring to it.

Leo Tolstoy said, "The greatest quality a writer can possess is the quality of mercy." But what does that mean? We must begin, I suppose, by defining the word. According to the American Heritage dictionary, *mercy* (Latin *merces*: reward) is kind and compassionate treatment of a person under one's power. Mercy emphasizes compassion in a general way; it suggests reprieve from a fate of considerable severity, without further implication.

This is an interesting definition, but it strikes me as not quite right. (I'm a show runner. I give notes.) The word *mercy* takes on another nuance when used in the context of creative writing. We do not offer "reprieves" to our characters. When we are merciful toward them, we simply agree to see the humanness in them, regardless of their actions.

It is often said that writers become godlike when they begin to maneuver their creations around in a sea of prose or stage directions. I believe this is true insofar as it offers us a glimpse of how God must feel when free will causes us to spin off in some unfortunate direction. He marvels at our choices, no doubt. Sometimes, I swear I can hear the sound of God's palm slapping his forehead in amazement and frustration. (By the way, I'm aware that God probably has neither a palm nor a forehead; this is a metaphor. Stay with me.) But he does not discount, discard, or dismiss us. He never stops seeing us as we are: human beings created in his image. We are the ones who constantly insist on dehumanizing each other. And we do that when we deny that fallibility is part of the human condition, when we refuse to admit that we are all in the same soup. Or as Bruce Springsteen once put it, "waist deep in the big muddy."

Because I am a writer, I am in love with semantics. I believe, as Shakespeare put it, in finding the right word, not its first cousin. We have declared ourselves writers, not preachers. When I go to church, I want to hear a preacher. I don't want to hear someone equivocating on moral issues, leading me into the gray areas, throwing up his hands and saying, "Who knows?" I want someone who can assert a system of beliefs, a moral code, a way of being. I want someone with some answers, some advice, or at least a persuasive argument. But when I pick up a book or go to see a movie or turn on the television, I want something else. I want to read poetry, see art, experience the acute observation of human nature, without any forced conclusions.

The Hebrew word for salvation means "to make wide." What does this mean in terms of modern interpretation? In the most literal, religious sense, it means that the path of forgiveness or salvation is wider than we can imagine. It makes room for mistakes, absorbs and absolves them. For the writer, it means something else. The person who devotes himself or herself to a religious order agrees to follow a narrow path. But the writer must follow a wide path. He must consider everything. He must observe it all, and if he is wise, spiritual, or even ambitious, he will attempt to recognize God in the most godless places.

The Roman poet Terence said, "I am human; I do not think of any human thing as foreign to me." Unfortunately, people often misinterpret this quote as an invitation to hedonism. But Terence is not saying that everything should be experienced. He is simply putting forth the argument that every act of human nature, even the extremes, connects us in some vital way. It's all to be considered. When we see acts of extreme heroism, our hearts fill up and we feel proud of our species and reassured by the actions of others because we see our own natures reflected in their choices.

By the same token, when we hear about the latest John Wayne Gacy or Jeffrey Dahmer, it is our instinct to declare such a person "an animal." We wish it were true. We wish we could distance ourselves in a significant way, something more definitive than brain chemistry or the random configuration of environmental circumstances. But the truth is, we can't. The truth is, these people who commit such deeds are not animals. They are human beings. And we are forced to claim our connection to them just as certainly as we are to beloved friends, to brave leaders, to martyrs, and to saints.

The fact is, we cannot confront the concept of mercy without confronting the reality of sin. Mercy does not, need not, exist without sin. I have often heard Christian writers say that they avoid reading or viewing certain material because they just don't want to know, just don't want to think about these things. This might be an option for the average person. This is not an option for writers. The writer is obligated to look under every rock. He can and should reject certain behaviors or choices in his personal life. But he cannot avoid contemplating the entire spectrum of the human condition.

When I was working on *Moonlighting*, there was a legendary story floating around about a freelancer who came in to pitch to the show's creator and executive producer. In a rather bombastic tone, the freelance writer said, "This is a story about good and evil." To which the executive producer replied, "Oh, good *and* evil." I am fond of this story because it has very much to do with my recent conversion to Catholicism. I had been dabbling in the contradictory worlds of yoga and spiritualism and self-help and intellectual cynicism. A New

Age California climate of, "Hey, it's all good." The idea was simply not to acknowledge the negative. Give it no authority. But the negative does have authority, and one of the quickest ways to empower it is to pretend it does not exist.

Then came the events of September 11. I remember staring at the TV screen and thinking, "Oh, good *and* evil." Up till then, I had been someone who could not choose God until I understood every aspect of him and what he was up to. In that moment, I decided to go ahead and choose God and worry about the details later. I was relying on a philosophy that a devout Catholic had offered an agnostic friend of mine: "Maybe what God is doing is just none of your business."

Kathleen Norris, in her wise and beautiful book *Amazing Grace*, quotes one Father Martin Smith on the subject of John Keats's theory of negative capability. He identifies

> a widespread need in contemporary spirituality to find ways of praying and engaging with God, our selves and one another, that have room for simultaneous contradictions, the experience of opposite emotions. We need to find the sacredness in living the tensions and to admit how unsacred, how disconnecting and profane, are the attempts at praying and living while suppressing half of the stuff that fascinates and plagues us.[1]

The writer simply cannot take the chance of suppressing those aspects of life. The Christian cannot take that chance either. When I go to Mass, I manage to transcend the ugly contradictions of being alive and in the world. By the time I reach the parking lot, that's pretty much over. Even so, it is an hour and a half more of peace than I used to get every week. Like most people, I want the world to be manageable. I want it to stay still and make sense. But the writer in me knows that such a world would not be worth observing, let alone worth tolerating an agent for. As Kathleen Norris puts it, "If we seek a God we can handle, that will be exactly what we get. A God we can manipulate, suspiciously like ourselves, the wideness of whose mercy we've cut down to size."[2]

I believe we get the same results if we insist on viewing or writing a world we can handle. If we insist on a portrait of the human condition that is manageable, full of easy victories and obvious wrong choices, we will not only cheat ourselves in the artistic arena—providing and consuming boring and superficial entertainment rather than art—but we will deprive ourselves of a deep, true, complex, meaningful awareness of God.

When I was writing my novel *Close to Home*, I decided to create a character who would be defined by nothing more than the fact that he was bad. I made him destructive to others as well as to himself. I made him selfish, narcissistic, insensitive, compulsive, and devoid of conscience. What's more, I decided not to give him any psychological reason for his behavior. He was not abused or neglected. He was simply bad.

This all worked well until I got to the very end of the novel when I was supposed to kill him. I realized that two things had happened. One was that I loved him. The other was that he was not, despite all my best efforts, entirely bad. I discovered that he had managed to keep a very important secret for the story's protagonist, who was as good as this character was bad. He had made a single sacrifice early in his life that had had an enormous effect. It was, in fact, his one selfless act. He had done one good thing.

According to quantum mechanics, everything is connected. You cannot pick up a coffee cup without affecting the weather somewhere. Every bad deed reverberates. But so does every good deed. Everyone has done one good thing. And that makes every life valuable. Certainly it makes every life indelibly connected to another. This is why no person can be called an animal and nothing human can be foreign to us. Kathleen Norris says, "To reject the world is to reject other people. And to reject other people is to reject Christ himself."[3]

Another way to exhibit mercy in your writing is by breaking through cultural, ethnic, and socio-economic stereotypes. If we insist on depicting unwed mothers or people struggling with addictions as evil, poverty as the catalyst for all crime and abuse, broken homes as the cause of all our ills, and people who have not found their faith as the fly in the cosmological ointment, then we are going to find ourselves wading through a superficial world indeed. And worse, one which bears no resemblance to the truth.

Writing is a beautifully mysterious process. We get to know the feel of controlling our own universe, and we get to know the feel of having that control taken away from us by the free will of our own creation. While we are writing, we are able to glimpse the way we should be able to live—fully aware that we are all connected by the same basic laws of physics and metaphysics.

On an ordinary day, I have trouble remembering that. On an ordinary day, I am someone who imagines that God feels exactly the way I do about people who talk on cell phones in restaurants. I am certain he has a special punishment planned for men in Porsches, the creators of *Survivor*, and actors who write novels. But when I work, those shortcomings fall away, and I find myself capable of forgiving the most unforgivable deeds, of seeing myself in the most unrecognizable character, of seeing God in every human encounter. It doesn't stay with me for long, but the ability to see it stays with me, and I struggle to revisit it whenever I feel alone, cut off, alienated. Most of all, I struggle to revisit it whenever I am feeling superior, whenever I find myself taking up residence in God's hip pocket, whenever I believe that I know more and deserve better. If nothing else, writing affords us the gift of humility.

Graham Greene summed up the concept of our creative spiritual dilemma in a passage from his beautiful novel *The Power and the Glory*. It goes like this:

> The wall of the burial ground had fallen in; one or two crosses had been smashed by enthusiasts: an angel had lost one of its stone wings, and what gravestones were left undamaged leant at an acute angle in long marshy grass. One image of the Mother of God had lost ears and arms and stood like a pagan Venus over the grave of some rich forgotten timber merchant. It was odd—this fury to deface because, of course, you could not deface enough. If God had been like a toad, you could have rid the globe of toads, but when God was like yourself, it was no good being content with stone figures—you had to kill yourself among the graves.[4]

This is the challenge and the frustration of writing. This is the gift of it too. And to take pen to paper or to turn on the computer in an effort to commit art is to be faced with the terrible beauty and the dangerous complexity of being alive. Observe it all, good *and* evil. Know that human behavior mostly falls in between the cracks.

This is why we cannot simply dismiss our flawed characters or glorify our worthy protagonists. We must strike a balance. We must remember that the truth is what we are after, and the truth is complex. It is hard to pin down, difficult to define or to recognize, hard to hear.

Along these lines, I offer a beautiful reading from 1 Kings 19:

> [Elijah] traveled forty days and forty nights until he reached Horeb, the mountain of God. There he went into a cave and spent the night. . . . The LORD said, "Go out and stand on the mountain in the presence of the LORD, for the LORD is about to pass by." Then a great and powerful wind tore the mountains apart and shattered the rocks before the LORD, but

the LORD was not in the wind. After the wind there was an earthquake, but the LORD was not in the earthquake. After the earthquake came a fire, but the LORD was not in the fire. And after the fire came a gentle whisper. When Elijah heard it, he pulled his cloak over his face and went out and stood at the mouth of the cave.

So it doesn't matter if your writing is loud or passionate or forceful or important. Without mercy, it is just noise. And mercy is in the whisper.

Sincerely,
Barbara Hall

---

**Notes**

1. Kathleen Norris, *Amazing Grace* (New York: Riverhead Books, 1998).
2. Ibid.
3. Ibid.
4. Graham Greene, *The Power and the Glory* (New York: Viking Adutt, 1946).

# 13 What Kind of Stories Should We Tell?

## Linda Seger

Among the legions of hopeful screenwriters, there are none more well-intentioned than Christians. Christian writers want to communicate hope, possibilities, a world redeemed and characters transformed. Yet, the Christian writer is often caught in a dilemma that is rarely a concern of other writers. What exactly is their mission as Christian writers? Are they to use their work to communicate the gospel, telling the audience about Jesus? Are they to communicate the possibilities of redemption and transformation? Should their work be explicitly, or implicitly,

Dr. Linda Seger created and defined the job of script consultant when she began her business in 1981. Since then, she has consulted on over two thousand scripts, including over forty produced feature films and about thirty-five produced television projects. Her clients have included TriStar Pictures, Ray Bradbury, William Kelley, and production companies and writers from six continents. Dr. Seger is an internationally known speaker in the area of screenwriting, having lectured in over twenty countries. She has given seminars for studios, networks, production companies, television series, and film commissions. She is the author of eight books, including *Making a Good Script Great* and *Creating Unforgettable Characters*. She has appeared on more than sixty radio and television shows, including National Public Radio and CNN.

religious? Are they to tell socially uplifting stories? Or to show the triumph of the human spirit? Or the triumph of good over evil? Or the ultimate triumph of God's love?

## Should They Create a Prescriptive or Descriptive Story?

A writer must decide to create either a descriptive or a prescriptive story. Most Christians want to create a prescriptive story, showing how things *can* be. They focus on hope and redemption, and the potential and promises of the spiritual life. They tell stories of transformation, specifically, of people changing as a result of their relationship with God.

This presents its own set of problems. Many Christians begin with redemption, rather than end with it, in the sense that they are determined to get there, whether the character's story has earned a redemption or not. Instead of showing the process people go through to find God, these writers are eager to show the result. They sometimes tend to make everything pretty and nice. They forget to show the struggle, pain, resistances, obstacles, and courage needed to turn to the Christian life. In trying to create the prescriptive film, they often leave out the drama. They forget the difficulties they themselves went through, and focus on the wonders of finally finding Christ. In their zeal to show where we can get to, they write stories that minimize how we got there.

How can they get around this? First, it's essential to recognize that drama is about process. It's about the stages of growth, and the movement through those stages. From a story standpoint, it means understanding, and remembering, the process of transformation.

For many Christians, this is difficult to do. Their impulse is to convert others, and their instinct is to do it through words. They quote the Bible. They tell their own stories of conversion. They debate the existence of God and the problem of

154

evil. The method through which they fulfill their evangelical mission is verbal: debate, discussion, formulas, sermonizing, chatting, and sometimes hanging out and shooting the breeze. In the worst cases, they can become preachy, overly rational and logical, and unfeelingly dogmatic. Their desire to fulfill their mission by using the techniques of the word can actually cause them to become superficial and skirt the deeper issues that truly would communicate the Word and the Spirit. But even at their best, all of these methods are essentially undramatic.

To spread the Good News through film, Christian writers will have to learn a whole new series of techniques. Nothing is as deadly on screen as talk, talk, talk. Drama is about action, not talk. An engaging movie focuses on what characters do in the story and what they experience, not what is said to them.

Ironically, much of the Gospels shows Jesus doing essentially dramatic activities. He healed. He accepted. He confronted. He acted and caused reactions from others as a result. He also reacted to others' choices, creating what we in Hollywood call momentum and a story line. He was pushed and pleaded with and prodded into action. He was spat upon. He was whipped. He was tormented. He was crucified. All of these are highly dramatic actions, which led to emotional reactions from him and from others. The power of his actions created powerful emotional responses that transformed those who encountered him. Film viewers can be transformed in the same way by witnessing a compelling character's dramatic choices.

**Embrace the Descriptive Drama?**

The descriptive film is intrinsically more dramatic than the prescriptive film. Descriptive projects find their starting places in the complexity of individual and societal evils, and so they are immediately more compelling for an audience. But there are pitfalls for Christian storytellers here too.

For a Christian writing the descriptive film, the intent may be to make an argument for the social gospel. These writers appropriate Jesus's mission to free those in bondage, to give sight to the blind, and to create a more harmonious and balanced world. They often put the focus on right action rather than right belief. This doesn't mean that they consider belief and faith to be unnecessary to the Christian life, but in the process of trying to use drama in essentially dramatic ways, the transformations that occur in these films may not seem overtly Christian, but may, instead, be a transformation to goodness, compassion, kindness, sensitivity, and change. Many Christian writers, and readers, will ultimately find this kind of story unsatisfying in its mere humanism.

Further, in striving to flesh out a descriptive tale, Christian writers very often produce work that is nothing as much as a wallowing in how awful things are. They showcase the dark and the evil in life and hope that the audience will move on from the horror to how much we're all in need of redemption. In so doing, Christian work can end up reading just like the work of a non-Christian: dark, angry, transfixed by the spectacle of sin. In reaching for this kind of edgy commerciality, many Christian writers end up compromising their fundamental vision and are never able to raise their stories out of the muck to a transcendent level.

## Stories with the Best of Both Worlds

It is possible for the Christian writer to have the best of the descriptive and prescriptive worlds. This can be expressed by creating the transformational arc.

People are transformed by events. Things happen to us that change us. It can be the death of someone close to us that makes us question God, and we either become closer to or more distant from him. It might be the presentation of a great blessing that makes us eternally thankful to the Divine Spirit who so clearly loves us that we have no choice but to respond with gratitude and a new commitment of life. It might be the opening of our minds that comes from travel or new friendships. It may be a profound crisis where our need for God was so tremendous that we knew for the first time the truth of our innate dependency.

The storyteller's task is to create events around a character that are so strong they can't be ignored. These events will force a reaction from a character and from the audience who will make the transforming journey with that character.

We are also transformed by other people. People do not transform us by giving us advice and a good talking-to. They transform us by entering into a dynamic relationship with us, which can be a negative or positive experience. We may be transformed through another's anger, disappointment, betrayal, criticism, or mean-spiritedness. Or else we may be changed through another's care for us. We can be overwhelmed by their compassion and rendered strong through a sense of their love. And we can know, as we experience the wonders of human goodness, that we have been touched by the Spirit of God. These moments of grace are dramatic. It is the writer's job in a transformational story to find them, to express them honestly, and to allow them to sing.

These moments are neither sentimental nor sappy nor superficial, but they're often rendered this way in film. These moments fail dramatically when the events and choices that elicit these responses in the characters do not elicit the same responses in the audience.

Film can be a particularly good expression of our Christian values and theologies, because it is an art form that unfolds through a process, just like spiritual transformation. A movie story and its characters never stand still but play out in a dynamic sequence of moments. This gives the Christian writer the opportunity to play both sides of descriptive and prescriptive drama. The writer can begin with the descriptive, moving deeply into the shadow side of life that truly needs to be redeemed. Whether it's portraying the individual's need for redemption or the need for social redemption, drama can convey the truth about the current state of one's individual and/or social context. It can define and show the problem. It can show the mess of things. It can show why something has to be done.

Then, by creating a transformational arc, drama can show the possibility of change, and how and why people are able to change. Since drama is a visual medium, writers need to learn how to *show* change, as achieved through irrevocable choices. A writer can show what the change looks like, again through the new choices that a character makes as the story progresses.

## Play the Subtext

Preaching is an overt action. You say what you mean. You tell it like it is. You come at it from different angles, telling stories, parables, examples, giving pithy statements, all the time trying to make it very clear what you're trying to communicate.

Drama is about subtext. It's about hiding as much as you reveal and saying less rather than more. It's about filling a sentence with layers of meaning and the willingness to be mysterious. It's about recognizing the truth of human communication that we often don't say what we mean, and we often try to disguise our true feelings and our true attitudes.

Drama does not pound; it nuances. It does not attack directly. It approaches the idea surreptitiously. It's not about making everything conscious, but instead about glimpsing the unconscious.

This means that the Christian writer has to be willing to suggest rather than tell. The Christian writer has to be willing to give the viewer choices, knowing that the film might be only one step in the audience's transformation. The story might lead rather than convince. It might nudge rather than lead one to a final decision. But if done well, it will reach within the hearts of the audience and touch a center of free will that offers them a new way of thinking and feeling, a new way of judging, a new possibility of being. There are other gardeners whose job it is to do the rest.

### Subtext Is Powerful but Imprecise

A film need not be explicitly Christian to communicate a Christian worldview and Christian ideas and ideals. In the same way, because film works on a subtextual level, sometimes the underlying message is either unclear or communicates something quite different from what the writer wants to communicate. In fact, sometimes Christian writers actually communicate non-Christian ideas without intending to.

We may all get different messages from a film because we're reading the film on different levels. Although the film *Braveheart* was written by a highly respected Christian writer (Randall Wallace) and many consider its message to be a strong theme of justice, I had trouble with the theme of the film because I felt it was also communicating the idea that "the best defense is a good offense" and "violence resolves problems." Some Christians had trouble with the film *The Associates* because Whoopi Goldberg's character had a friend who was gay and other friends who were considered the outcasts of society. I thought that the movie carried a strong Christian theme of the kind of community that Jesus talked about—people being accepted and loved in spite of the fact that they carry different burdens of sin. There have been tremendous controversies

159

about such films as *The Last Temptation of Christ, The Passion of the Christ, Left Behind, Jesus of Montreal, Broken Vows,* and *The Third Miracle,* among others. Some consider these films heretical, or anti-Semitic, or not theologically sound. Others find them powerful and faith-based.

Why does this happen? Because theology and drama are multileveled and subtextual; it's easy for inaccurate theological ideas to be communicated. I have worked on religious scripts in which the writer thought he was communicating a loving God, and I saw a vengeful God instead. Sometimes the writer thought he was communicating a God who saves, but I saw a God who saved some and killed off others who seemed to be expendable. Sometimes writers communicate a God who loves those who are socially acceptable and rich but who rejects those who are outcasts. This may be done unwittingly, but these layers of information do come across.

When writers are working with strong theological material, they must make sure there are other theologians to advise them about underlying meanings that may be coming through. Although I have two master's degrees and a doctorate in theology, I know that I may not catch all the layers of meaning and the nuances of theology in a particular project. Sometimes I question a theological idea but want to make sure that I'm not reading something into the script.

Drama, like any medium, has limits. With it, you can influence lives, you can change attitudes, but you may not change belief systems. You can affect feelings, but you may not move someone to action. If your intent with drama is to force change, you may decide that this isn't the right medium for you, since great drama leaves the audience free to choose and doesn't try to manipulate. Or you may decide that you want to work with drama in conjunction with other art forms or other mediums, allowing the discussion or sermon to do the reflective part and the drama to do its active part.

I have been fascinated with drama since I was a very small child. I have loved its ability to express values, to communicate the human condition, to combine all the arts together in this most collaborative of all art forms. Since the age of twenty-one, I have been studying drama and theology, both separately and together. The Christian community would do well to embrace both, seeing in each a complementary intersection that is most profound, wise, and natural.

# 14      A Filmmaker's Progress

## Scott Derrickson

This essay is adapted from a speech delivered in Los Angeles at the 2003 "Mere Entertainment" conference, sponsored by Fuller Theological Seminary and Act One.

Bob Dylan wrote the song "Times They Are A-Changin'" in 1967 to depict the cultural upheavals of the time, but his lyrics also quite accurately describe my sentiments toward certain transformations occurring these days within the church of God. There is a major shift happening within Christ's church, and it is fundamentally a generational shift. Cultural analysts call this a shift from modernity to postmodernity, and the visible result is a widening ideological chasm between older Christians and the new, younger generation of believers. The differences in the philosophies of these two generations are

Scott Derrickson is the director and co-writer of *The Exorcism of Emily Rose*, starring Laura Linney and Tom Wilkinson. He was co-writer of *Urban Legends: Final Cut* and co-writer/director of *Hellraiser: Inferno*. He worked with Wim Wenders, co-writing the story for the German director's latest film, *The Land of Plenty*. He has written films for Disney, Dimension Films, Jerry Bruckheimer, and Martin Scorsese, among others.

uniquely evident in how each approaches the integration of faith with art and entertainment.

I am, I think, an older member of this new generation of Christian artists and entertainers who seem to be rejecting old paradigms in favor of new ones. My intention today is to describe my own ideological transformation, and I think this is pertinent because I've met many young Christians who are now traveling down the same philosophical paths that I did.

I graduated in 1990 from Biola University and afterward went to film school at USC. After that, in 1996, I began working as a writer/director in Hollywood, and I've been working nonstop ever since. As I made this journey from high school, through college, and on into the film industry, I often felt like the character Christian in *The Pilgrim's Progress*. John Bunyan's wonderful book is an allegory of the Christian life and features a main character, Christian, who carries a burden on his back—the burden of his own sin. Christian roams the earth looking for relief, which he eventually finds at the foot of the cross. During much of the last decade, I too carried a burden on my back, but it was not the burden of my sin. I had become a Christian in high school, and that weight had been lifted. What I carried during my journey toward a filmmaking career was the burden of a question: what is the duty of a Christian in Hollywood?

My ideological journey began in a place I'll call the Village of Passive Consumers. It is home to most people in our culture; the vast majority of Americans reside in the Village of Passive Consumers. Citizens of this place mindlessly absorb art and entertainment with very little critical thought. I grew up in the Village of Passive Consumers—and I'm very glad that I did, because the people who live there love movies. Growing up, I saw hundreds of films, and though my friends and family never dissected or discussed the meaning of what we watched, it was there in the Village of Passive Consumers that I fell deeply in love with cinema. In fact, I came to love movies so much that I wanted to become one of the people who get to write and direct them. I decided I would leave the Village of Passive Consumers and head off to the faraway land of Hollywood, where I hoped to one day become a filmmaker. But as soon as I decided to take this voyage, I felt the burden of this question: what is my duty as a Christian in Hollywood? I immediately sought relief, but of course, no one in the Village of Passive Consumers had a clue. Nobody there could answer my question.

With the burden still on my back, I began the journey toward the land of Hollywood, and as I traveled along, I came upon a group of Christians I'll call the Battalion of Value Changers. This was a militant group of believers who spoke in militaristic terms. They saw themselves as soldiers in God's army, and they often spoke of "conquering Hollywood for Christ." To the Battalion of Value Changers, Hollywood was the enemy, and their mission was to inject mainstream movies with Christian values. This was essentially their answer to my question; this, they told me, was the primary duty of a Christian in Hollywood.

What I admired about this particular group of believers is that of all the Christians I encountered on my journey, they took their faith the most seriously. They were anything but lukewarm. These individuals would rather take a bullet to the head than risk violating their conscience or contaminating their devotional life. I'm grateful to have been influenced by the intensity of their passion and the sturdiness of their faith.

However, as I spent time with the Battalion of Value Changers, I actually began to miss the Village of Passive Consumers, because it became increasingly clear to me that the Battalion of Value Changers didn't really love movies. Most of the battalion, it seemed, didn't even know a good movie from a bad movie. What seemed to drive these militant Christians was the unspoken conviction that the movie medium itself does not inherently glorify God. To them, art and entertainment were not to be appreciated for their own sake, but rather, art and entertainment were strictly weapons in the culture war. These Christians were consumed by an "us versus them" mentality toward Hollywood, which was something I never understood, and eventually I was compelled to reject their mission altogether.

To me, the basic endeavor of the Battalion of Value Changers was marked by a decidedly non-Christian approach to creativity. To enter the creative process with such a prescribed agenda and with the arrogant confidence that you have the antidote to cultural ills seemed like a surefire recipe for the creation of propaganda rather than quality art or entertainment. I began to feel more affinity with writers like Walker Percy, Madeleine L'Engle, and Flannery O'Connor—writers whose method of integrating faith and devotion with creativity seemed more humble, more authentic, and ultimately much more powerful. Flannery O'Connor wrote, "The Christian writer does not decide what would be good for the world and then proceed to deliver it. Like a very doubtful Jacob, the Christian writer confronts what stands in his path and wonders if he will come out of the struggle at all."[1] To me, that seemed to be a more Christian approach to creativity. To create is to prostrate yourself before the work itself and to submit to the likelihood that the work will change you, not that you will change culture through the work. My own experience with creativity had already proven that my creative endeavors could quite easily level my intentions with ruthless truth and challenge my thinking and behavior. So, in the end, the Battalion of Value Changers did not help relieve my burden. They did not answer my question.

With no relief, I ventured on and eventually came across the Content Assassins—another militant group, though not as zealous as the Battalion of Value Changers. The Content Assassins were a small, educated band of Christians who took careful aim at Hollywood movies, then shot holes in their non-Christian content. Targeting mainstream movies, these people sought to inform the church about the secular worldviews that underlie popular art and entertainment. I owe a lot to the Content Assassins, because they taught me how to think more critically about cinema. They were the antithesis of the Village of Passive Consumers—they watched movies with their eyes wide open, carefully evaluating what they saw from a theological perspective. They deeply enriched my ability to look beneath the surface of films, and thereby greatly enhanced my understanding of cinema.

The more conservative members of the Content Assassins had created watchdog periodicals that rated the acceptability of a movie by its quantity of sex, violence, and profanity. The more thoughtful members focused on the underlying ideology of a film. While there is some real merit to the work of the Content Assassins, I found myself increasingly frustrated with their decidedly negative outlook on cinema. Like the Battalion of Value Changers, they viewed Hollywood as the enemy, and therefore had a fundamentally negative approach to film. Their first thought when evaluating any given movie was to expose what was wrong with it.

This approach made me bristle, because I preferred that my first response to any person or any creative work be to discover what is right and good, not what is wrong or undesirable. This different tendency of response is a significant part of the new generational chasm in the church—young Christians, for the most part, are far less interested in criticizing a non-Christian person's point of view than in seeking out how that person's point of view may be a resource for some truth. Rather than fixate on how a secular work of art or entertainment may violate or contradict their beliefs and convictions, young Christians, for the most part, would rather discover how it can connect to their faith and possibly even inform it.

The Content Assassins not only focused on the negatives of almost any given film, but they also were constantly shooting holes in movies that I dearly loved. I grew more and more convinced that even if a movie has a fundamentally anti-Christian aesthetic or ideology, this does not necessarily mean that it ought to be dismissed. I love the films of Ingmar Bergman, even though they communicate an idea that is absolutely anti-Christian—that God does not exist, or if he does exist, he is silent. Regarding the presence of God in the world, I couldn't disagree more, but Bergman's films are so beautifully made and so honestly capture his experience in the world that I am deeply moved when I watch them. He made his films with great humility, trying to share what he felt about the world, and I find in those films a deep connection to that part of me that doubts—that part of me that wrestles with my faith like Job, Nehemiah, and even Christ. Rather than criticize or reject Bergman's work, I gratefully embrace it as something that is deeply human and greatly enriches my life. This kind of positive, celebratory outlook on cinema was something I had possessed since my years in the Village of Passive Consumers, and I didn't want to let it go. So the Content Assassins did not answer my question; I still didn't know my duty as a Christian in Hollywood.

I went on my way, and the next place I stopped was the Purple Heart Hospital. This was a place for wounded members of the Content Assassins and the Battalion of Value Changers who had actually been to the land of Hollywood. Once there, they had each been fired from a job or had turned down a job because of their Christian moral convictions. These people were casualties in the culture war, and now here they were, laid up, licking their wounds, reveling in their unemployment for Christ. I met a guy there who was quite proud of the fact that he had written a television script that contained such heavy Christian content that it inspired his producer to throw the script across the room. I met a director who smiled up at me and gloried in the fact that he was fired from a big studio movie because of his refusal to compromise a scene. I met a girl who boasted to the press that she had turned down a lucrative job to write a horror sequel because it violated her Christian conscience. While I greatly admired the willingness of these believers to pay the price of their convictions, I found their proclivity to boast about it rather reprehensible. And behind all the boasting, I ultimately felt as though they were encouraging me to go out into all of Hollywood and fail for Jesus. It became immediately apparent that the Purple Heart Hospital held no relief for my burden, so I quickly moved on.

Continuing down the path, I came to the Monastery of Harmless Entertainment—a place for Christians who are devoted to living a life insulated from the world. The believers in the Monastery of Harmless Entertainment had a very clear and precise answer to my question: they told me that my duty as a Christian in Hollywood was to create art and entertainment that is above all innocuous and harmless. They told me that my Christian duty was simply to increase the quantity of non-offensive material in the marketplace. I sympathized with these people because most of them were concerned parents. I myself have a young child and am concerned that he will be overwhelmed by exploitive material in the media marketplace. And of course, I love a good G- or PG-rated movie as much as a good PG-13- or R-rated movie.

Nevertheless, what began to disillusion me about the Monastery of Harmless Entertainment was that they advocated the rather ludicrous idea that G- and PG-rated material is inherently superior in moral quality to PG-13- or R-rated material. They thoroughly believed that family-friendly material is intrinsically of higher moral value than R-rated material that explores darker truth. I found this to be totally incongruent with the texts of Scripture. The story of Noah and the ark—a story that you can tell in any child's Sunday school class—is not of higher moral value than, say, the story of David—a man so consumed with lust that he commits murder and steals his victim's wife. Even more "R-rated" is the story in which David, who, wanting another woman, Saul's daughter, slaughters two hundred Philistines, cuts off his victims' foreskins, then puts them on a plate and brings them to King Saul. That's not a family-friendly story. I doubt that you'll ever see a Sunday school flannelgraph of bloody foreskins. Nonetheless, that was a story God saw fit to include in the canon of Scripture, and I certainly don't believe that it is of lesser moral value than the story of Noah and the ark.

In time, I realized that the convictions of those within the Monastery of Harmless Entertainment were contrary to my own. Unlike most of them, I don't believe the moral quality of a movie can be determined by its MPAA rating. So, having found no answer to my question, I left the Monastery of Harmless Entertainment.

The next place I discovered gave me a bit of relief. The Uplifting Movies Theme Park was a place I genuinely enjoyed, and so I spent quite a bit of time there. This is a place that celebrates and promotes movies that are positive and uplifting. The first thing I noticed about the Uplifting Movies Theme Park was that it was owned and operated by believers who truly loved and celebrated cinema. They didn't view Hollywood as the enemy. They loved movies like *Chariots of Fire*, *It's a Wonderful Life*, and *To Kill a Mockingbird*. To my surprise, I learned that they even appreciated some R-rated movies like *The Shawshank Redemption* and *Schindler's List*. These are all excellent movies that are marked by uplifting values, sympathetic characters, and positive themes.

At first, I really enjoyed these people because I could relate to their love for movies, but as I spent more time with them,

I began to feel a lack of affinity with the Uplifting Movies Theme Park. I grew disturbed that the people here were unwilling to celebrate, appreciate, or promote many of what I considered to be the best movies in the history of cinema. They certainly wouldn't celebrate *The Godfather*, *Taxi Driver*, or *The Exorcist*. I also began to see that many of the movies that they were celebrating and promoting reeked of facile transcendence and cheap sentimentalism. Perhaps this was an issue of taste more than anything else, because I love truth in the dark. There is some real darkness in me, and I'm drawn to stories that grapple with that darkness, then seek to find illumination within it. This is why I work primarily in the horror, thriller, and science-fiction genres; those genres are often about truth in dark places. At the Uplifting Movies Theme Park, however, no darkness is allowed. I appreciated the place, but it most certainly did not answer my question for me; it could not tell me my duty as a Christian in Hollywood.

As I continued my journey toward Hollywood, my burden grew heavier, and eventually I became exasperated with all the Christian misconceptions about art and entertainment. Out of shameful desperation, I joined a group that helped me find temporary relief from the burden on my back. I joined the Eff-You Gang. This was a small, ragtag group of outlaw believers who, like me, had grown weary of the hypocrisy and self-righteousness of the church, and they enabled me to find temporary relief for my burden by simply ignoring it. Those of us in the gang loved to sit around and mock conservative Christians and their insidious small-mindedness. We smoked a lot, drank a lot, and swore a lot, because it was our Christian liberty to do so.

I am now a bit embarrassed to have been a part of the Eff-You Gang, but I am grateful to them for helping me to discover my true liberty in Christ. They enabled me to feel mercilessly free from the opinions of others. I had a lot of fun with this gang, but over time my heart grew hard in their presence. I became increasingly cynical, and my devotional life ground to a halt. What drove this group was resentment, and eventually I saw that harboring resentment is like swallowing poison and hoping that someone else will die. Furthermore, I learned that resentment against the church is a uniquely dangerous thing; it is both immoral and unwise to resent the bride of Christ. Eventually, I returned to my senses and stopped ignoring God's divine calling in my life. I left the Eff-You Gang, picked my burden back up off the ground, confessed my sin, found mercy, and ventured on alone.

As I approached the land of Hollywood, I encountered two more groups on the outskirts. The first group, the Covert Christian Movie Companies, were actually getting movies made, and I saw that as a remarkable thing for anybody to do. These believers felt that the duty of a Christian in Hollywood was to make non-evangelistic, mainstream movies that featured a certain quotient of understated Christian content. Most of their movies would have at least one character who was a Christian, and often that character would spontaneously pray or talk about God during the movie. The problem with most of these films was that they were failing financially, and the reason for their failure, I think, was that the Christian content stuck out like a sore thumb. To sprinkle a little bit of Christianity over a mainstream movie is a bit like sprinkling jalapeno peppers over a bowl of cereal.

As I watched the movies made by the Covert Christian Movie Companies, I usually found the Christian content to be incredibly awkward and jarring; it was usually incongruent with the rest of the film. The root of the problem, I came to realize, was that the people who worked for these companies were ultimately motivated by guilt. They did not believe that making a good mainstream movie for its own sake was justifiable; only the presence of Christian content justified the endeavor. To these believers, spiritualizing a movie was what made it unique and worth pursuing. They felt that slipping Christianity into a mainstream film was their duty as Christians in Hollywood. The problem was that their movies simply didn't work.

I am not implying, of course, that a good movie cannot feature Christian content. In fact, most of the movies I've written for studios deal very directly with faith and belief, and many great films have featured Christian characters or dealt directly with Christian ideas. *Signs*, *The Exorcist*, *The Apostle*, *Dead Man Walking*—these are all movies that are centered on faith-based themes and characters. The filmmakers who made these movies understood what the Covert Christian Movie Companies did not: to include Christianity in a mainstream movie is to feed the audience a hot pepper that is potent, powerful, and often quite complicated. These are spicy movies that delve deeply into spiritual characters and ideas, rather than trying to covertly sprinkle them into the story. Personally, I don't feel at all obligated to write movies with Christian ideas or characters of faith. They just happen to be what I like to write. The marketplace these days is certainly not resistant to movies with Christian content as long as that content is organic to a well-told story.

The problem with the Covert Christian Movie Companies' films was that they felt to me like those posters of natural landscapes with Bible verses etched across the image. Those pictures always made me feel like somebody felt a little guilty, like the picture of nature itself was not quite glorifying to God, so they added the verse. I usually wish the verse wasn't there, because God's work in nature is inherently glorifying. It doesn't need to be spiritualized. The same is true about a good film; it doesn't need to be spiritualized to glorify God.

Also on the outskirts of the land of Hollywood was one more group—the Godsploitation Filmmakers. These folks were fascinating; they had created a new type of movie—the Godsploitation film. In the 1970s, a movement known as exploitation cinema was created by filmmakers like Russ Meyer, Roger Corman, and Jack Hill. They found a niche market for highly exploitative, low-budget, low-quality movies. The appeal of these films was that they guaranteed a target audience a certain amount of exploitative sex and violence. The audience for these films simply wanted to get their sex/violence fix, and as long as they got that, the rest of the low-quality movie material was fine with them. The Godsploitation Filmmakers were essentially doing the same thing, but they were targeting the church, and so rather than providing the audience with exploitative sex and violence, they were providing a cheap theological fix for conservative Christians who were fascinated by the impending apocalypse.

I have to give these filmmakers credit: most of their movies made money. These people had found a target market in the low-brow church, then created material that would capitalize on that market. Furthermore, the Godsploitation Filmmakers woke up Hollywood, and I think this is their great contribution to the church's role in Hollywood right now. The Godsploitation Filmmakers are responsible for making Hollywood aware that Christians actually watch movies and that there is great public interest in exclusively spiritual and religious cinematic material. But the actual films that the Godsploitation Filmmakers were making deeply disturbed me. First of all, these dramatizations of the apocalypse were propagating a dispensational eschatology that I fundamentally reject. Second, their films weren't any good. Third, the target audience was the Christian subculture, and I found that to be the most troubling thing of all. I knew that as a writer and director, I was not interested in helping to build a Christian film industry that paralleled the Christian music industry, where subquality talent would tickle the ears of an insulated subcultural church for a buck. So I tipped my hat to the Godsploitation Filmmakers and went on my way.

But I still had the burden on my back. I still had no answer to my question: what is my duty as a Christian in Hollywood?

Shortly after entering the land of Hollywood, I was hired to write and direct a movie. I became an employee, and suddenly my Christian duty became quite clear. I realized that my primary duty as a Christian in Hollywood is the same as the primary duty of the Christian at Microsoft or UPS or the police department. My primary duty as a Christian in Hollywood is to do my job well. I came to recognize that quality work is what both God and my employer require of me.

As I looked around, I saw that I wasn't alone. I saw, first of all, other Christians in Hollywood who were working as writers, directors, producers, and actors. And all of them had one thing in common: they put a premium on the quality of their work. Second, I discovered there was this new, young generation of Christians who had a unique and burgeoning interest in quality. They wanted to understand, appreciate, and participate in cinematic excellence, both as film viewers and as filmmakers. I joined up with these other believers and became part of a group that I'll call Quality Club.

If you want to work in Hollywood, you have to join Quality Club, because unless your work is excellent, you'll never make it. To be employed as a full-time studio writer or director is comparable to getting into the NBA; it's that competitive. Can you imagine the ludicrousness of a guy who says he wants to get into the NBA to become an influence for Christ, to share the gospel with other players, or to decrease bouts of violence in the game but doesn't put in the time or effort to become exceptionally good at playing basketball? How absurd! That guy is never going to play in the NBA. Likewise, Christian writers and directors must, above all, dedicate themselves to excellence in their craft. Signature

Bible verses for Quality Club members are Colossians 3:23, "Whatever you do, work at it with all your heart, as working for the Lord," and Proverbs 22:29, "Do you see a man skilled in his work? He will serve before kings; he will not serve before obscure men."

Quality Club, like Fight Club, has rules. The first rule of Quality Club is to do excellent work. Excellence in your craft earns you a place in the industry, and continued delivery of excellent work is what ensures your future employment. Looking back at the Christian groups I encountered during my journey into the land of Hollywood, I see that the fault line running through all of them is that they did not prioritize the quality of their creative work.

The second rule of Quality Club is to do marketable work. If your work isn't marketable, it will never get made. Furthermore, if you're hired to work on a film, and the work you deliver is not marketable, you will not continue to be hired in the future. Studios pay me to write movies that will earn them a profit, and when I agree to take a job, I am obligated to do what I have been hired to do. If I write something that is not marketable, then I have failed to do quality work for my employer.

The third rule of Quality Club is to work with moral integrity. By this rule, I simply mean that you must demonstrate quality in the process as well as the product of your work. Moral integrity demands, first and foremost, that you service your employer well. It is morally questionable to seek the subversion of your employer's business with covert Christian motives, and it is morally objectionable to fail to deliver what you are paid to deliver.

Moral integrity also demands that you treat people with love, honesty, and respect. Hollywood, unfortunately, is a place that often rewards bad behavior, but a Christian must avoid such behavior nonetheless. You can't scream at people on the set. You can't lie to get what you want. You can't stand in self-righteous judgment of people who are different from you. You can't be motivated by fame or money but only by what you believe God would have you do. You cannot create material that you believe will have a primarily detrimental effect on the audience, and by this I mean that you cannot be involved in the creation of material that will fundamentally move the audience away from what Plato and Kierkegaard called "the Good." Moving people toward the Good is the privilege and opportunity of the Christian artist, but it is not always an obligation. Excellence is the obligation. If a television commercial director is hired by Schick to sell shaving cream, his obligation is to demonstrate excellent craftsmanship and create a commercial that sells shaving cream. But those who work in the dramatic arts often have the unique opportunity and privilege to move people toward the Good.

For the Christian in Hollywood, excellence is the constant obligation, moving the audience away from the Good is the forbidden practice, and moving people toward the Good is the unique opportunity to be taken whenever possible and appropriate. Excellence, marketability, integrity—these are the rules of Quality Club, and quality work is the primary duty of the Christian in Hollywood.

**Notes**

1. Flannery O'Connor, *Mystery and Manners* (New York: Farrar, Straus, and Giroux, 1969).

# 15 We're Just Like You . . . Really!

## Jack Gilbert

During the 2004 presidential election, many liberal commentators portrayed the "Religious Right" in terms ranging from patronizing to outright demonizing. Many of my Christian friends were justly angered. But I find their ire to be somewhat ironic. This is exactly how these same Christians describe people in Hollywood—calling them everything from immoral morons to sinister co-conspirators with the devil himself.

It's not hard to understand why Christians, or anyone else for that matter, see Hollywood as the "other." Nightly shows like *Entertainment Tonight* and *Extra* and even an entire cable channel like *E!* slavishly follow the foibles and excesses of entertainment royalty. Along with Brad Pitt, Barbra Streisand, and Michael Eisner, however, this book's

Formerly the workshop director of the industry's most prestigious and successful television writing program, the Warner Bros. Writers Workshop, Jack Gilbert is currently coordinator of Act One's TV Track. He has been a freelance reader for the William Morris Agency, NBC, and MTM Productions, and has consulted on projects ranging from *Batman Forever* to *The Addams Family*.

other contributors and I are also members of the Hollywood "other."

Is it really so strange that Christians would be a part of the Hollywood community? Even if Hollywood *is* the new Babylon, remember that God asked some of his people to take part in the daily life of *old* Babylon:

> Build houses and settle down; plant gardens and eat what they produce. Marry and have sons and daughters; find wives for your sons and give your daughters in marriage, so that they too may have sons and daughters. Increase in number there; do not decrease. Also, seek the peace and prosperity of the city to which I have carried you into exile. Pray to the LORD for it, because if it prospers, you too will prosper.
>
> Jeremiah 29:5–7

I may not have had plastic surgery, several marriages, or a wing named for me at the Betty Ford Clinic, but I have been a part of this business for almost twenty years. I've read over a thousand movie and TV scripts, looking for talented new writers, and have almost as many shares of worthless AOL/Time-Warner stock options to show for it.

What follows is not a scientific survey but the results of a two-decade observation of what goes on both inside and outside of Hollywood. This essay's purpose is to show that the differences between the rest of the world and "Hollywood insiders" are far fewer than our commonalities. At our core, we're just like you—only more so. Take the best and worst of humanity, boil it down to a stew of dreams and ambitions, fears and insecurities, and you have Hollywood.

Now, of course no one wants to deny there are differences. For instance, we have more than our fair share of attractive people out here, thanks to our many actors and actresses (and their supporting personal trainers, makeup artists, and plastic surgeons). As you can imagine, someone who isn't at least a bit adventurous and willing to take risks isn't likely to end up out here. We have a Han Solo–like disregard for the odds, and we live on the edge. For example, many of us balance our checking accounts via the ATM; when the ATM stops dispensing, we stop spending.

We also have more than our share of driven, type-A personalities. If it's not agents and executives compensating for a lack of physical stature with an overabundance of drive or producers armed with their stainless steel thermal coffee mugs (designer water is apparently out), it's the legions of determined or desperate actors descending on the next teen horror movie casting call. Hollywood attracts so many go-getters because only here can a winning personality and a great script or a perfect look put you on the road to fame and fortune.

### We Started Out Like You

It's easy to think that we grew up at movie premieres, learned to read from screenplays, and now live exclusively with people who've been interviewed by Barbara Walters. But in the first place, America's hometowns are *our* hometowns. Hollywood has produced some notable offspring like Michael Douglas, Jamie Lee Curtis, and Drew Barrymore, but the vast majority of us are first-generation immigrants to Tinseltown.

I notice this especially around holidays as I hear wistful reminisces about sledding down icy Connecticut hills, jostling to see the window displays at FAO Schwarz in New York, or strolling among the warm glow of luminarias in Santa Fe. We all have our favorite regional foods too, from Philly cheesesteak to crawfish gumbo to brats. If you want to get a fight started, forget politics; just ask which city makes the best pizza. And one of the reasons there isn't an NFL team in the country's second-largest TV market is because so many of us already have our team loyalties, from the Packers to the Cowboys, the Yankees to the Red Sox, the Cornhuskers to the Fighting Irish.

## We Want to Be Successful

Even if you are not in the habit of reading the tabloids at the checkout stand or tuning in to the Oscars early to hear Joan Rivers gush over gowns and jewelry, it is easy to get the idea that Hollywood's definition of success is about money and fame. In our hearts, though, what we really want is for our lives to add up to something. We all want to feel like we matter. What I hear often is that people here want to do something really wonderful, something truly excellent. Our heroes are the actors, directors, writers, and technical people who have managed to achieve that consistently.

For a time, my office at Warner Bros. was right across the hall from the writers' room for *The Drew Carey Show*, known for its goofy and sometimes raunchy humor. Deborah Oppenheimer, one of its producers, was well compensated for her comedic efforts, but she poured her heart into an Academy Award–winning documentary on the Kindertransport—German Jewish children sent to safety in England by parents who later perished in Nazi concentration camps.

We are much more likely to envy a person with an Oscar or an Emmy than someone in a box office smash. That's why it's not unusual to see big names in very small but very passionate projects. Glamorous Charlize Theron transformed herself into a tortured serial killer in *Monster*. Comedian Bill Murray gave the performance of his life as a burned-out actor in *Lost in Translation*. And as unlikely as this might seem from what's on TV and at the cinema, the projects we are most enthusiastic about are those we think will make our children proud of us.

## We Want to Be Appreciated

While sports celebrities and rock superstars are beginning to compete with Hollywood celebrities for the title of "most vain," the perception is that Hollywood is *the* place where people with insatiable egos go to find unheard-of recognition and unrestrained adulation. The praise and attention heaped upon Hollywood celebrities may reach absurd extremes, but the underlying desire for acceptance that fuels this absurdity is universal the world over.

We all need to know that we matter, and it's no different in Hollywood. The difference here is how unevenly appreciation is doled out. For most, years of numbing rejection are the rule.

Even at the most basic level—getting paid for your efforts—appreciation is hard to find. On any given day, of the writers who already have been successful enough to sell a script, less than 5 percent are working. Of members on the Screen Actors Guild, the number probably drops below 1 percent. When I lost my position at Warner Bros. after a ten-year run, I received genuine but muted sympathy from my friends. Can you blame them? The majority of them had averaged a job a year during the same period. And as those of you who have been "between jobs" know, the loss of self-esteem is compounded by the rejections you face looking for your next job.

A produced writing team slaves for a year on a script for a big action film only to have studio executives get cold feet when a much-hyped blockbuster opens to mixed reviews and mediocre box office receipts. An actress who has worked steadily for twenty years now finds she's losing even bit parts.

On the other hand, for a very small few, appreciation comes in such an unimaginable volume that it is often overwhelming. For most people, being in the spotlight means holding the top spot in their fantasy football pool or displaying a new "Student of the Month" sticker on their car. For some celebrities, it means they literally can't go anywhere in the world without being recognized. Fame often comes suddenly, massively, and out of proportion to one's actual contribution to society.

## Group Think

When a bunch of the same type of people end up in the same place, it shouldn't come as any surprise that they end up thinking a lot alike. Just as it's almost impossible to find a Michigan Wolverines fan in Ohio during the month of November or *anyone* in Boston who doesn't claim to be Irish on St. Patrick's Day, so do those of us in Hollywood who eat and sleep movies and TV tend to see the world through the same semi-distorting lens.

Who doesn't eagerly await Monday morning to study the weekend box office numbers? Everyone certainly has their choice about who the next Batman should be. And doesn't everybody lose sleep worrying about what *Survivor* and *American Idol* are doing to actors and writers?

Just as farmers see everything through the cycle of their crops and Little League dads get carried away when their sons get called out at home plate, so we in Hollywood lose perspective and end up buying into the very publicity we create.

## Living Down to Expectations

I've noticed a tendency among people in Hollywood to live up (or down) to the expectations people put on us. Just as the school troublemaker finds it easy to behave like his label, we seem to embrace the image projected on us. And if by some chance we happen to become successful, a whole new set of expectations comes into play.

Welfare mothers live under one set of expectations; high-powered corporate execs live under another. Celebrities have inherited their own. The press gives frenzied coverage to celebrity weddings along with predictions of how soon the couple will be in divorce court. So in spite of the myth that we create our own realities out here, our realities more often than not seem to bear a suspicious resemblance to the stereotypes. Such expectations do not excuse us from taking responsibility for our own decisions any more than they excuse gangbangers or stockbrokers. But these expectations may help explain some of the behavior in Hollywood.

## The Tyranny of the Now

Another way Hollywood is much like the rest of the world is that while everyone here is thinking about the next big thing, most of our energy goes into making it through today. Our lives are dominated by the struggle to get the next part, sell our first script, or pitch even one saleable cable idea. We're competing for jobs with hungry film school grads willing to work for nothing just to get the experience. We're two days short of qualifying for next year's medical insurance.

As a result, idealism takes an unwitting backseat to pragmatism. Without realizing it, days turn to years, and the truly wonderful is often lost to the merely necessary.

One frequent question from the general public is, Why does Hollywood put out so much junk, from the merely unentertaining to the downright offensive? People in Hollywood are their own worst critics. You have only to hear a Hollywood audience groan during the trailers or listen to a pack of Hollywood insiders gleefully dissect M. Night Shyamalan's latest film to be convinced of this.

But we also realize there are a thousand ways a good project can come up short. Believe me, no one starts out wanting to make a rotten movie or a failed TV show. Besides being hard on the ego, flops are hard on the career. And no one out here but people

185

like Oprah Winfrey, Julia Roberts, and Clint Eastwood have anything resembling university tenure or a guaranteed union job. In fact, this fear of failure sometimes unintentionally contributes to the very thing we're trying so desperately to avoid.

J. K. Rowling can spend as long as she likes writing the next installment of *Harry Potter*, but *CSI* has to come up with twenty-two stories every season, then produce them on weekly deadlines. And the multiplexes demand a continuous supply of new movies to keep their seats filled and their concession stands busy.

The people I know out here want to produce material that matters. Unfortunately, the market is limited for many of those projects. Couples on a date night almost always go for entertainment over enlightenment. And from the looks of what audiences are voting for with their remotes, it's unlikely that America would watch night after night of issue-driven drama on network TV.

So what do we do? We tell ourselves that in order to be able to survive in this business long enough to make our magnum opus, we just need to make this one formula horror film or humiliating reality show. After all, we tell ourselves, all we're doing is trying to get a couple of extra laughs from not-so-subtle innuendo, just pushing a boundary or two so we won't be seen as old hat. It's only one small movie, we say, only a couple hours of forgettable television. Really, what's the harm?

But of course, the cumulative effect of many people making the same decision all over town becomes anything but harmless. We fail to realize that the guy at the studio next door is in the same position, and that we're both like the woman in the studio down the street who made the same decision for the same reasons a month ago.

From the outside, it may seem like Hollywood has hatched a strategy to dumb down the American public or to entice its youth into irresponsible and possibly harmful behavior. But the reality is less an intentional conspiracy of the malevolent than an unwitting series of similar choices. The effect may be the same, but the intent is not.

## Bad Behavior

And what about the behavior or misbehavior of us Hollywood types? People tend to think Hollywood is all parties, drugs, and sex. To some extent, we bring this perception on ourselves. Sometimes it seems like half of us in Hollywood are employed by biopics, exposés, and celebrity pet shows about the other half. But for many, when movies or television shows are in production and eighteen-hour days are the norm, we crave a good night's sleep more than anything else. If it weren't for movie openings, Oscar parties, or political fundraisers, most of us would never leave our apartments.

The opportunity to live to excess becomes a possibility only when one of us gets a big break and becomes the next hot thing. The years of "paying our dues" do little to prepare us to cope with the deluge of fame and fortune. Like many lottery winners, we have a difficult time with the sudden wealth. And once we arrive, we find ourselves taking our cues from those who are already there. We fall back on the same instincts as everyone else. We act the part celebrities are allowed to play. Ironically, the public may be shocked at an arrest for DUI, disorderly conduct, or cocaine possession, but such an arrest almost always results in greater popularity.

Near the end of the Richard Curtis script for the romantic comedy *Notting Hill*, a movie star, played by Julia Roberts, has come back to Hugh Grant's travel book shop in Notting Hill to apologize for behaving, well, like a movie star, and to ask if they could try one more time. To her surprise and dismay, his reply is a judicious no. His Notting Hill can never live up to her Beverly Hills, and she can't be any more famous than he is forgettable. She reluctantly agrees, but as she leaves she

187

lets him know that she's "also just a girl. Standing in front of a boy. Asking him to love her." It takes the uncensored honesty of Hugh Grant's mad Welsh flatmate and the gentle nudging of his close friends to help him realize she was right and deserving of a second chance.

But that's in the movies. Many of us out here don't have nearly the self-awareness or wonderful turn of phrase that Richard Curtis's movie star had. Regardless, she isn't speaking just for Hollywood celebrities but for the same need for love all human beings have.

Like you, although we in Hollywood share the same desire for a life that counts and the same need to be appreciated, we also struggle and often settle. We settle for thinking just like the next guy, acting out parts others give us, and letting selfish ends justify questionable means.

We're in need of a second chance we don't deserve and a love we can't comprehend. And if that's true, we're just like you . . . really!

# 16     Love the Cinema, Hate the Sin

## Jonathan Bock

I know that in movies these days, the only people who read the Bible are serial killers and yokels. I know that Hollywood usually portrays Catholic priests as alcoholics or child molesters. I've heard entertainment execs claim that sex and violence in movies have no effect on audiences (though, somehow, they simultaneously maintain that product placements do). I know all these things very well, but here's the problem: I love movies.

I love a crowded theater on a Friday night, a tub of popcorn with salt and butter (the real stuff, not that venomous oil). I

Jonathan Bock is the founder and president of Grace Hill Media, a public relations firm that is committed to raising awareness among religious Americans of entertainment that shares in their beliefs, explores their values, and enhances and elevates their view of the world. Clients of Grace Hill Media include Universal Pictures, Warner Bros., Paramount, New Line Cinema, Fox, Columbia Pictures, ABC, NBC, CBS, PAX, MGM/UA, and Disney. Mr. Bock began his career in publicity at Warner Bros. in Los Angeles. Prior to that, he was a sitcom writer. Currently, Jonathan serves on the board of Reel Spirituality at Fuller Theological Seminary and is an advisory board member for Inter-Mission, an entertainment-based ministry.

love the anticipation as the lights go down, the bellows of laughter or the brutal jeers as the previews roll. And then the opening strains of the score break in, the first images flicker on the screen, and for the next two hours, hundreds of complete strangers become comrades, lost in the unfolding story.

To quote Yogi Berra, "I love movies when I like them." And I suspect you love them when you like them too. How do I know that? Box office grosses are at an all-time high. DVD and home video sales and rentals continue to skyrocket every year. And in poll after poll, the esteemed sociologist George Barna reaffirms Christians go to movies *at the exact same rate* as the rest of the country.

That's right; for all our moral outrage, Christians love movies as much as everyone else. To borrow from the film *Network*, we may go to the window and scream that we're "mad as hell and not going to take it anymore," but we'll be back in front of the tube in no time.

Hollywood. We might love to hate it, but we love it just the same.

### Can't Take Our Eyes off You

This is why so many of us feel conflicted, sometimes even guilty, when it comes to watching movies. We don't want to give tacit approval for the harmful things we see in them. And we don't want to support an industry that at best doesn't share our values and at worst attacks us for holding those values. But what do we do? Movies, both at the cineplex and in our homes, have become part of our everyday lives.

In his fine book *The Struggle for America's Soul*, Robert Wuthnow crystallizes the issue:

> The problem is in being true to our own religious convictions—holding them with passion—and yet knowing how

to behave in public life, where we must interact with people who do not share our convictions. Like it or not, movies have become an inescapable part of our public life. The question we must ask is no longer just "what do we do about Hollywood?" Now we must also ask: "How do we live our faith in a Hollywood world?" Or to put it yet another way: How can we love the cinema, but hate the sin?[1]

For years our answer has been to complain about Horrible Hollywood and then shrug our shoulders and continue to shell out our money at the box office. In the meantime, Hollywood has continued down the same tawdry trail, and we have continued to be conflicted.

There's a better way. Not only can we love the cinema while hating the sin, but in doing so we can radically transform Hollywood. Sounds pretty far-fetched, right? It's not. We *can* live our faith while still being part of public life. And in doing so, Christians will not only alter how the entertainment industry portrays us, but we will also create a respectful rapport with it. Plus, if we do what I am proposing, we will also change how Hollywood does business by exponentially increasing the number of Christian writers, directors, and producers. And we'll change the culture for the betterment of everyone—all while more fully living out our faith.

What is this ambitious plan?

Go to *more* movies.

Yep, that's it. Go to more movies. No boycotts. No press conferences. No marches. No posters or flyers or mailers or phone calls. No sit-ins or blockades or protests or picketing. None of that will work nearly as effectively as heading off to the matinee at the theater. The conflict between Christians and Hollywood will be resolved not with the pen or the sword, but with our seats.

How can I be so confident that people of faith can really turn Hollywood around simply by going to more movies?

Because of one incredible statistic: according to the Gallup Organization, 43 percent of Americans (over 120 million people) attend a church service every Sunday.[2] Christians are a gigantic, if unreliable, market. If we begin attending more films, we will become the largest moviegoing market in the world. Of course, that's a big "if," so let's get down to details.

## The Ratings Game

With all due respect to my fellow authors on the radio or television side of the business, I propose that we focus all of our attention on the movie industry. Television and radio are ratings-driven; film is driven by sales. In TV and radio, success is determined not only by audience size, but the age and gender demographics of those listening or viewing. Based on that information, the outlet will then determine a rate to charge advertisers for commercial time.

Frequently, a TV show can have high ratings but be a weak income producer. An example of this strange paradox is the hit *Murder, She Wrote*. Although consistently ranked in the top ten, *Murder, She Wrote* had a core audience outside the eighteen through forty-nine demographic, whose sponsors pay the most money to reach with advertising. Despite having much lower ratings, competing shows on other networks had the favorable demographics and were able to collect double the fee that CBS garnered from *Murder, She Wrote*. Ultimately, that was the main reason for the show's cancellation.

The Nielson and Arbitron ratings systems are also based on estimates of households that might be tuning in, not on actual concrete numbers. In truth, they're nothing more than sophisticated surveys founded on remarkably small samplings of viewers and listeners. Compound this with the myriad number of stations and markets, and the number of real viewers becomes widely diffused and complicated to verify.

The movie business, however, is not based on ratings or advertising. Success is determined solely by ticket sales. To Hollywood, it's all about getting butts in the seats. What's more, the studios and theaters don't really care who buys the tickets, just so long as they buy them. Age is unimportant. Gender is inconsequential. Whether you're nine or ninety-nine, as long as you regularly plunk down your hard-earned cash, they're happy.

This method of measuring success plays perfectly into our strength—which is our numbers. The sheer volume of people we can deliver to the box office can transform an under-performing film into an enormous success. Think of it. If only 5 percent of the 120 million Americans who go to church every Sunday decided to see a particular movie, then those 6 million people would roughly add *45 million dollars* to the gross take of that film. Trust me, that'll get the folks at the studios to sit up and take notice.

It also means we can make *any movie we want to* into a hit.

## The 90 Percent Rule

It's easy to see the power Christians could wield if they saw a certain film en masse. But divisions will undoubtedly arise in deciding what kinds of movies we should see. Should we see only religious films, or are some secular films acceptable? What if the movie has nudity, violence, or bad language? What if it's a good film, but it stars an actor whose personal life is less commendable?

Primarily, we should target films that share and uplift the core virtues—films that elevate the human spirit, call men and women to achieve goals and live by principles bigger than themselves. Most important, they should be films that, while they may never invoke his name, are sprinkled with the trail markers that point the way to God.

For those of you who have problems with language, sexual situations, or violence, going to films above "G" is always a dicey proposition, and supporting films that have any of these elements can be a hard egg to order. So here's my solution, something I call "The 90 Percent Rule." As long as a movie has 90 percent of what you'd want, support it. No film is going to be 100 percent perfect to 100 percent of the people. (Just ask 10 people what their favorite movie is, and I'll bet you get 10 different answers.) So live by the 90 percent rule and just wince through the rest.

## Opening Is Everything

As a movie marketer, I'm well aware of the importance of a film's opening weekend. And for Christians to have influence in Hollywood, you need to understand its importance too. Opening weekend is the barometer by which Hollywood measures success. If a film earns a lot of money in its first three days, nothing else matters. It's a hit, and the industry will immediately scramble to make more films like it.

The opening box office also plays a lucrative role for the future of that film property in ancillary markets. If a movie opens big, then cable and television networks begin negotiating for the broadcast rights based on a percentage of that initial success. And don't think the folks at Wal-Mart and Target aren't paying attention to the first weekend when considering which film properties get the best shelf locations. All of this is influenced by that first three days. So if we're going to have any real effect at all, it's going to require hitting the cineplex early and en masse.

## Hollywood's Dirty Secret

There is another significant but rarely acknowledged reason for making films that share our values into enormous hits. It goes right to the core fear of any sentient studio executive. It's something they certainly don't want you to know, something they wouldn't even confess to their closest filmmaker friends. It's Hollywood's dirty little secret: nobody knows for sure how to make a hit. That's the ugly truth. I might end up with a bloody horse head between my sheets, but now you know.

Oh, for sure, accomplished filmmakers and executives think they know the *ingredients* that go into making a smash: big-name star, high-concept story, deliciously evil villain, great release date, funny trailer, etc. But with absolute certainty? No way. That's why you see so many copycat movies coming out after an original success story. On Monday morning, studio heads read about the boffo numbers on a competitor's film, call a staff meeting, and scream, "Get me a WWII epic!" or "Where's my teen slasher film?" Ask yourself: if they really knew how to make a hit movie, why wouldn't they do it every time?

If Christians would go as a demographic block to a movie on opening weekend, we could make that movie a hit. And the studios would make more films just like it. We would wield the power that Hollywood execs would kill for: to know in advance which movies will be hits.

Money is the altar at which Hollywood worships. It's the Alpha and Omega, the holiest of the holy. In truth, there's not a studio in town that wouldn't put a test pattern up on the screen if you'd pay nine bucks to watch it. Consider this quote from Michael Eisner, chairman of the Disney Company: "We have no obligation to make history. We have no obligation to make art. We have no obligation to make a statement. To make money is our only objective."[3]

Isn't that wonderful news? Dear Christians, we should be breaking out the champagne and celebrating our victory! We've already won! We don't have to combat prejudice. In Hollywood, the only industry-wide bias is to make money. We don't have to fight against institutional anti-religious intransigence. We don't have to battle different philosophies, principles, or creeds. Hollywood only wants our money. And since we're 120 million strong, money is one thing we have plenty of. I say we gladly give 'em what they want.

## A New Renaissance

"So," might say the skeptic, "I see what's in it for Hollywood, but what's in it for the body of Christ? They get to line their pockets with our hard-earned money, but what do we get?" It's a fair question.

First off, we get respect. If Christians show up in droves, Hollywood is going to go out of its way to avoid offending their cash-cow audience. That means you're going to see fewer alcoholic priests, Bible-thumping hypocrites, and lecherous televangelists. We'll also see a newfound aversion to using God's name in vain, because their research departments will tell studio executives that those expletives "don't trend well."

Second, we'll get more of the movies we like and less of the ones we don't. Every studio has a finite number of films they're going to make in any given calendar year. So, for example, Warner Bros. makes roughly 30 films a year. Let's suppose that in the last year, they made 2 films that shared your values. If both of those films had made 150 million dollars, trust me, next year they'll make more. Now, they're not going to make 30, because they have other kinds of films that also make money, like action films and slasher films. But they might make 4. And if the other studios see the trend in finding success in values-laden, elevating films, then all of the sudden you have 30–40 films in that category every year. Not bad. It's important to note that we're not going to see films with gratuitous violence and sex disappear altogether. Hollywood knows those films make fairly consistent money too. But because there's a limited pool of films that get made every year by the studios, *there will be 30–40 fewer films that don't share your values.* More of the ones you want, less of the ones you don't. That's how you start to shape culture.

Third, and perhaps most significant, over several years our labors will reintroduce the church to mainstream culture. We as Christians have basically abandoned mainstream arts and entertainment over the last several decades. What a disgrace! We of the lineage of Michelangelo, Raphael, Shakespeare, Lewis, Tolkien, and Caravaggio. There was a time when Christians were the undisputed masters of art and literature. Where are the masters now? Instead of slogging it out in the rough and tumble environment of pop culture, we Christians have instead created our own subculture of Christian radio, books, television, and film. Mainstream culture has moved on without us, and the world of entertainment has coarsened in our absence.

If nothing else, our presence will hopefully shore up the levee and hold back the tide of debauchery and gratuitousness, until a new generation of Christian artists can offer the world a new Renaissance as an alternative to the lowest common denominator.

Changing Hollywood will require two virtues Christians habitually lack—patience and persistence. We'll need to set our eyes on the long-term prize of righting the ship of mainstream culture by bailing it out one bucket at a time. But we'll get there, and one day in our lifetimes, the world will marvel at our great works once more.

---

**Notes**

1. Robert Wuthnow, *The Struggle for America's Soul* (Grand Rapids: Eerdmans, 1989).

2. Gallup Organization poll, December 1994, quoted in George Bishop, "What Americans Really Believe," *Free Inquiry*, Summer 1999, 38–42.

3. Gregory McNamee, "Disney War," *Hollywood Reporter*, February 16, 2005.

# 17     A View from the Top

## Donovan Jacobs

For Hollywood's decision-makers, everything comes down to three questions: "How cheap can we make it?" "How many people will watch it?" and "How much will it gross at the box office?" I've been working with executives at movie studios and TV networks for twenty years, and I can't think of one instance when the decision to make a film or series didn't depend on the answers to these questions.

Christians deserve credit for trying to get Hollywood to think about more than its pocketbook. We have rightly insisted that executives take responsibility for what they foist on the public. But too often our tactics have had the opposite effect, reinforcing the suits' obsession with the bottom line.

As a development executive and script consultant for numerous motion picture production companies and television networks, including Warner Bros., ABC, Touchstone Pictures, and Walden Media, Donovan Jacobs helped create a wide range of theatrical films and movies for television. He specializes in the development of family movies for television, working on the Humanitas Award–winning *Ruby Bridges* and *Eloise at the Plaza* for *The Wonderful World of Disney* on ABC. Donovan is a graduate of the prestigious Warner Bros. Workshop for television.

It's time for a new plan of action. But first, we need to understand how executives operate.

Executives tend to be wary of movies and TV shows with overtly spiritual themes, and not for reasons you might expect. About ten years ago, I worked as a story analyst for Hollywood Pictures, a division of Disney. I was assigned to read a script that posed the question: what if Jesus returned to Earth in the body of a teenage girl in Santa Barbara? I gave it a minor rave. I loved its sense of humor and its audacious premise, which I thought could stir some healthy controversy and help promote the film. And I emphasized that the material wasn't trying to proselytize. (As I recall, the writer was Jewish.) What I didn't tell the studio was that I was personally thrilled that a movie based on the screenplay might open some hearts to Christ's message and encourage much-needed public discourse about religion.

The executives who read my report panicked. It had only been a few years since the release of *The Last Temptation of Christ*, and the furor that that movie had enflamed in the Christian community was still fresh in their minds. They immediately rejected the project and gave me a none-too-subtle warning to express less affection for spiritually themed projects. To the best of my knowledge, the screenplay has never been produced.

Because of the way Christians have reacted to projects like *The Last Temptation of Christ*, executives see spiritual material as a risk. And even with the box office triumph of *The Passion of the Christ* and the critical success of *Joan of Arcadia*, that's a risk many are unwilling to take.

And what about less overtly spiritual movies and TV shows that have something meaningful to say? Executives aren't afraid of these—they are just plain indifferent to them.

The executives I've dealt with insist that audiences only want to be entertained. They are wary of investing time and money in projects that make viewers think too much or question their lives. I was working for Touchstone Studios (another division of Disney) in the late 1990s when it released *The Insider*, a movie about a whistle-blower in the tobacco industry. The movie featured a powerhouse cast, topped by Russell Crowe and Al Pacino, and critics gave it terrific reviews. At a staff meeting prior to its release, I heard one executive admit that the studio couldn't figure out how to market the movie. It was too complex, he complained, to sum up on a movie poster or in a fifteen-second TV ad. *The Insider* did poorly at the box office. Disney president Michael Eisner later admitted that he wished his company had never made it.

There are, of course, executives who defy this mind-set. I worked with an executive at ABC who created movies and miniseries for *The Wonderful World of Disney*. She saw her work not only as a way of supplying family entertainment to millions but also as a means of empowering young girls.

While executives may talk about wanting to make quality entertainment, most of the ones I've encountered have been more devoted to maximizing the parent corporation's profits. Eisner once claimed in a memo that his *sole* responsibility was to the company's stockholders. And who could blame him? Most people go into business to make money.

But imagine what movies and television would be like if executives paid more attention to the meaning of what they produce. For one thing, there's evidence they would be more successful. A friend who once worked in feature animation for Disney tells me that both Disney and Pixar thoroughly analyze the themes and values in their animated films. These companies realize that parents care about what their children learn from watching their films. They know that meaning affects their bottom line.

This is key. We can change the atmosphere of indifference at studios and networks by proving to executives that there is a large audience longing for meaningful entertainment, and that we consider what movies and TV shows say when deciding what to watch.

But instead of telling them what we want to see, Christians have only been vocal about what they *don't* like—sex, violence, and coarse language. The *Spider-Man* movies brilliantly explore the theme "With great power comes great responsibility." But I've yet to hear Christian groups congratulate Columbia Pictures, the studio that produced the films, with the same fervor that they denounce Warner Bros. for allegedly promoting occultism with the *Harry Potter* movies.

Most executives think they are adequately serving the Christian audience with the few G-rated movies released each year, non-offensive family shows, and the occasional holiday movie and TV special. They don't believe there's a sufficient audience to justify a broader range of material with Christian-friendly themes, even though these themes have contributed to the popularity of entertainment as varied as *The Shawshank Redemption* and *Touched by an Angel*.

A Christian group trying a different approach is Paulist Productions, which for the last thirty years has awarded the Humanitas Prize to TV series and movies that "enrich as well as entertain." The mission of Humanitas is to "encourage those who create contemporary media to use their immense power in a humanistic way." In the process, the Humanitas has opened a dialogue with the networks and studios on exploring ideas that glorify God and uplift the human spirit.

---

There's an ugly ritual that occurs at TV networks a dozen times a year, when execs gather to decide whether to cancel a series. A senior executive at ABC told me about one such meeting in 2003 to kill off the show *Veritas*. A victim of poor ratings and worse reviews, *Veritas* seemed doomed until a single letter from a fan—possibly, my co-worker joked, the *only* fan of the show—caused those at the meeting to rethink cancellation. The executives overcame their fit of indecision, and *Veritas* was dumped. But the incident shows that letters to TV networks do wield power, even letters about shows that seem to be lost causes.

Yet while some letters have clout, others do not. Complaints about offensive subject matter often fall on deaf ears, particularly if the movie or show under attack is popular.

Christian groups have too frequently responded with boycotts, which simply don't work. One of the most famous was launched in 1997, when the Southern Baptist Convention urged its members to avoid all Disney products. The boycott was a response to a slew of controversial movies Disney had backed, like the ultraviolent *Pulp Fiction*, and the alleged "homosexual agenda" behind the decision to make the title character of ABC sitcom *Ellen* a lesbian. You would imagine an organization the size of the SBC, which claimed 15.7 million members in 2000, would have some clout. But over the last 7 years, the boycott has had no impact on Disney's creative or business policies. (Just a couple of years after the boycott began, I met a Touchstone executive who hadn't even heard of it.)

Protests and boycotts have been especially ineffective when they target things executives believe boost their bottom line. The networks have flat out ignored criticism of increased swearing on TV. Executives believe their shows must be racy to attract young adults, a demographic that doesn't watch much network TV but has plenty of disposable income, and to stem the loss of viewers to cable networks, where more graphic language is allowed. Many respected writers and producers, such as *NYPD Blue* creator Steven Bochco, claim to use swearing for authenticity, not to shock or get cheap laughs.

That doesn't mean Christians should muzzle their concerns. But we could be wiser in how we fight our battles.

Consider one of the more influential media advocacy groups in Hollywood: GLAAD, the Gay and Lesbian Alliance Against Defamation. Many Christians might not share GLAAD's desire to facilitate wider acceptance of gays and lesbians in society, but they could do worse than to implement the organization's media strategies.

Let's say a sitcom were to feature a stereotypically corrupt, sex-crazed fundamentalist preacher as a regular character. Instead of protesting the network, we could pinpoint specific scenes from the program that contain clearly gratuitous elements—ideally, examples that might garner attention from the news media. Like GLAAD, we could then offer suggestions, in a nonconfrontational tone, for how the network could make the program more authentic—and more sensitive to Christians.

In order to do their jobs, executives must have a penchant for saying no. Executives hear thousands of story ideas every year, and they read hundreds of scripts and books. Because they can only turn a fraction of these concepts into movies and TV shows, they look for a reason—any reason—to reject them. I've heard executives say a project is too expensive, it's not expensive enough, it can't be cast with a big star, it can't be described in one sentence, and somebody else is making a movie or show just like it. Just think: *E.T.*, *Home Alone*, and *The Apprentice* were all initially rejected. That's how eager execs are to say no.

The executives I've spoken to see Christians as negative people who won't watch even the most well-made shows because of one bad word or sexual reference. Their attitude is: Christians won't watch no matter what we make, so why bother making shows for them?

Boycotts and protests further antagonize decision-makers, who react by avoiding any subject matter that could invite criticism. The protests surrounding *The Last Temptation of Christ* convinced movie studios to reject religious projects for most of the 1990s. Even non-Christian material was affected. I worked with an executive at Hollywood Pictures who tried in vain to get the studio to adapt the best-selling book *The Celestine Prophecy*; perhaps they were afraid Christians would complain about the movie's New Age themes.

Out-of-the ordinary projects often have to find an advocate at the studio or network who will fight to get them made. A former co-worker at ABC spent over four years working to convince the network to produce and schedule *Dreamkeeper*, a miniseries that retold Native American myths. It finally aired in 2003.

Christian producers have made great strides recently in building relationships with studios and networks to get their projects made. But it would help if executives didn't think Christians were so picky. By watching more of what's already out there, Christians can help change this notion.

In particular, Christians should seek out movies and shows that don't fit the family genre in which Christians are so often pigeonholed. They should take chances on more obscure, independent movies like *Whale Rider*, a story about redemption and being chosen by God. And they could put aside some of their understandable reservations and check out the HBO series *Six Feet Under*, which, despite gay characters and graphic sex and violence, is one of the few shows on television to explore the varied religious lives of its characters. They could even take a second look at films like *Fight Club* and the Al Pacino version of *Scarface*, which, though brutal and graphic, are cautionary tales about material excess and spiritual emptiness.

In 1997, ABC premiered *Nothing Sacred*, a series about a Roman Catholic priest who struggles with his faith while facing dilemmas such as abortion and the ordination of women priests. Though the show received strong reviews, ABC badly mishandled it, pitting it against Thursday-night heavyweight *Friends*. Compounding the problem were protests by the Catholic League and other conservative Christian groups, who refused to give the show a chance because of some of its rougher edges. *Nothing Sacred* was canceled after one season, in part due to the very Christians who complain about the lack of spiritual themes on television. An opportunity to reach people with an intriguing version of God's message was lost.

When a project appears with as many good points as *Nothing Sacred*, Christians should support it, even if they aren't thrilled with the product as a whole. I'm not suggesting that we stop expressing our displeasure with objectionable material, but we *should* express ourselves in a way that won't cause executives to throw out the baby with the bathwater.

The current marketplace offers hope for Christians. Family movies continue to appeal to studios as well as independent filmmakers. Religion-themed best-sellers such as *The Da Vinci Code* and *The Purpose-Driven Life* are being adapted into major motion pictures. (On a smaller, but no less significant level, a friend of mine recently optioned his script about St. Francis to a pair of Catholic filmmakers.) And television will no doubt explore more spiritually oriented stories and characters in order to capitalize on the success of *The Passion*.

To build on this trend, the church needs to engage in constructive dialogue with the studios and networks, to be more positive so that the executives will say yes to good projects more often, and to take chances on programs and movies with a greater likelihood of entertaining a broader audience. Christ urged us to "fear not." We must urge executives to follow this advice while truly living it ourselves.

# 18 The $10 Billion Solution

## Charles B. Slocum

Described in the pages of this book are a number of promising strategies for changing Hollywood. Creative and business-minded Christians must become more successful in greater numbers with finer subtlety within the Hollywood system. The church must support evangelism of those in the industry who have ears to hear. Individual Christians in the audience must redirect their own day-to-day viewing to films and television programs that reflect their beliefs. These are all promising and necessary strategies, but they will all take time. Of course, the decade it will take to see significant results is but a second in God's eyes. But, there is a faster way to have an impact. It takes $10 billion.

Yes, billion with a "b." The entertainment industry is dominated by multibillion-dollar conglomerates; none are owned by a Christian. Buying into Hollywood takes billions of dol-

Charles B. Slocum is assistant executive director of the Writers Guild of America and chair of Act One's board of directors.

lars, but it would be money well invested, both financially and socially.

There certainly has been poorly invested Christian money brought to Hollywood. Two of my favorite films are *The Passion of the Christ* and *The Spitfire Grill*. Each had Christian intent behind them, were creatively successful, and earned large profits (though on two decidedly distinct scales) for their investors. They are also the two worst examples of how Christians should invest in Hollywood.

The reason they are poor examples for us to follow is that they were both single-film investments. I'm not an expert in the odds of winning a jackpot in Las Vegas, but I suspect that a single-film investment is just about as unlikely to return a profit. In fact, the Paul Kagan company, which advises Hollywood investors, conducted a study that showed that if you select a random slate of any five Hollywood films, the slate would typically be unprofitable. How could that be? Hollywood brings in billions! Yes, but Hollywood filmmaking is a game of odds. If the odds of a hit are one in twenty films, you better make twenty. In fact, as a business proposition you better make forty, or fifty, or sixty films. Only with the capital to last that long do the odds work in favor of the investor.

Scores of investors have lost billions of dollars by investing on too small a scale in Hollywood. The trade papers regularly report who is new in town with $100 million or $350 million or $500 million to invest in making and marketing feature films. Each name shows up 18 months, 2 years, or 3 years later as closed, bankrupt, or sold. Even legendary Hollywood independent film companies such as Miramax, New Line, and Orion have not been independent for years, having sold out long ago to deeper-pocketed conglomerates (Disney, Time Warner, and MGM, respectively). Indeed, even the venerable MGM (itself the combination of MGM and United Artists) recently sold to a larger company, Sony.

Christians have tried the strategy of investing on a modest scale. None of the efforts have succeeded for the long haul. Some good films were made along the way. But, a lasting footprint was not established.

This is no worse a track record than that of secular investors. Indeed, in recent decades in Hollywood, only one start-up company has raised money to invest in the making and marketing of feature films and survived independently. Just one. With Steven Spielberg and Jeffrey Katzenberg as their creative core, Dreamworks raised two billion. The massive size of their venture was surprising to many observers at the time. Now, it is unclear whether Dreamworks will succeed independently. Two billion dollars doesn't go as far as you might think.

This lack of success for new entrants is no accident. It is the result of a successful strategy by the incumbent studios to keep out new competitors. The heart of the strategy is to draw as much of the box office, DVD, and Pay-TV money as they can into as few films each year as possible. Each of the top studios will have films in the top twenty-five often enough over a period of about five years to earn back their losses on the failures. An undercapitalized new company will run out of funds in that same amount of time. This strategy to gang up on aspiring competitors is perfectly legal; no collusion need occur. Business strategists explain it with strategic group theory: a small number of incumbents acting independently, but along the same lines, to defend their turf. The self-protective choices are self-enforcing because any incumbent who strays from the strategy will fall victim itself. MGM suffered this fate.

In Hollywood, the general strategy, as suggested above, is to accentuate the hit-driven nature of the business. The film and television businesses are inherently hit-driven. This is caused by the nature of films and television programs as information goods, to use the language of economists. The primary characteristic of an information good is that it requires a large

211

investment to make the first copy and a very low cost to make each copy thereafter. If only a small number of consumers pay for the product, the losses are large because the high initial cost must be recouped. If the number of copies sold rises above the point where the initial investment is recouped, then profit rises dramatically and quickly; each additional unit sold is mostly profit.

The feature film version of these economics looks like this: a studio invests $50 million to make a film and $25 million to market it, for an upfront investment of $75 million. At the box office, 10 million tickets are sold for about $5 each, for total retail revenue of $50 million. The theater keeps about half, so the studio receives $25 million. When the theatrical exhibition window closes, the studio is still out $50 million. The international box office works the same way, but at about 60 percent of the amounts for the U.S. market, so the studio collects another $15 million; the loss is reduced to $35 million. Nine months later the studio releases the film on DVD and sells 4 million DVDs worldwide for a wholesale price of $10 each, for studio proceeds of $40 million. Suddenly the studio is $5 million in the black. Another $20 million will follow over the next 5 years from pay television, free television, and basic cable exploitation. Other costs will total $5 million. The studio has earned a total of $95 million in revenue on its investment of $80 million. The $20 million profit amounts to a profit of approximately 25 percent on the initial $75 million investment within five years, with the investment paid back within eighteen months.

That's a good business. But it can be dramatically better or worse easily and quickly. The initial $75 million is mostly gone before the studio knows if the film will succeed or not. Swings in profit or loss of tens of millions of dollars are a monthly experience for Hollywood studios. In a bad year, studio profits overall can swing hundreds of millions from the year before.

212

The general economic principles for information goods work in a similar way for television too. Think of it this way: the costs to get a television program on the air are the same whether one person watches or one hundred million people watch. The advertising revenues, however, go up or down based on the audience size. The fortunes of television companies, like their film colleagues, swing wildly with success and failure.

These economics have smoothed out somewhat with the assistance of several decades of technological developments. Films were originally dependent solely on the theatrical release for revenues; now DVDs and television follow. In television, cable networks carry repeats of even unsuccessful programs; these too are now selling on DVD.

But the single greatest strategy to offset the ups and downs of the economics of information goods is to own a lot of them. And the studios have gotten bigger.

Viacom is the combination of the National Amusements theater chain, Paramount Pictures and Television, Spelling Television, Big Ticket TV, Nickelodeon Cable, CBS TV Network, the UPN Television Network, MTV Cable Networks, King World Syndication Television, BET Cable, Showtime, Comedy Central, Westinghouse Broadcasting, Infinity Radio, Blockbuster Home Video (recently spun back out), and the TNN Network (now called Spike).

Time Warner is the combination of Time Inc., Warner Bros. Film & TV and cable, AOL, Castle Rock Entertainment, HBO and HBO Films, New Line Cinema, Turner Cable (TNT, TBS, CNN), Hanna Barbera, Lorimar TV, Telepictures TV, parts of the MGM and RKO film libraries, the WB Network, and Court TV.

Disney is the combination of Disney Film & TV (Buena Vista, Disney Channel, etc.), ABC TV & Radio, ESPN, Saban Entertainment, Miramax, Lifetime Cable, E! Entertainment Cable, A&E, and the History Channel.

NBC Universal is the combination of NBC TV, Universal Film & TV, Interscope Entertainment, Polygram Entertainment, October Films, Bravo Cable, MSNBC & CNBC, USA Network, Sci-Fi Network, Telemundo Network, and an interest in Pax TV.

News Corp. is the combination of 20th Century Fox Film & TV (FBC and the FX cable network), Regency TV, Greenblatt-Janollari, Cannell TV, New World TV, MTM Entertainment, Fox Sports, TV Guide, and the DirectTV satellite service.

Those mergers constitute horizontal consolidation—competitors combining. There has also been a lot of vertical integration within the industry—buyers and sellers combining into the same firm. All these combinations have made the entertainment conglomerates less and less vulnerable to the risks of the entertainment industry and made it harder for new companies to get large enough to earn the same protection.

Thus, we are returned to the beginning. For the church to get a running start at changing Hollywood, about $10 billion needs to be invested, mostly on acquisitions of existing companies. When Sony bought MGM for $4.8 billion, where was the Christian buyer? When News Corp. bought DirecTV from GM for $6.6 billion, where was the Christian bidder? When NBC bought Universal Studios and USA Networks for $5.5 billion, where was the Christian buyer? The chain of secular acquisition goes back twenty years in the contemporary setting, and dates, really, to the earliest days of Hollywood. There will be constant opportunities in the future. Lions Gate, a significant independent company, is currently looking for a buyer at a hoped-for price of $1.5 billion to $2 billion.

There have been several good starts at Christian investment on a large scale. Pat Robertson owned the Family Channel.

Bud Paxson created Pax TV. Gaylord Entertainment started TNN. But all these were sold from Christian hands into secular ones. These entrepreneurs could have followed the growth strategy modeled by Hollywood—both horizontally and vertically—so that these investments could succeed in Christian hands. But they didn't seek this battle. They were sellers, not buyers.

The best-thought-out Christian investment on a large scale is also the most recent. Philip Anschutz has bought up significant entertainment assets in Regal Cinemas and production company Walden Media. Still, Anschutz has taken some avoidable risks: he financed the production of the remake of *Around the World in Eighty Days* for at least $80 million with no distributor prearranged. When the movie failed at the box office, it likely wasn't Disney who lost money. He has done better with films such as *Ray* and *Holes*, but it is not clear that the investment in *Around the World* was part of a slate of films big enough to tilt the odds of having a hit in his favor. The best strategy for Anschutz would have been to buy either Universal or MGM. He is well-advised to get some like-minded investors together and spend about $5 billion more on well-chosen entertainment acquisitions over the next five years. That is the best way to ensure that the return on his investments to date pay off.

One more observation about Mel Gibson's investment in *The Passion of the Christ* is warranted: it was a charitable commitment of funds. Of course, with respect to IRS rules, it was not. But Gibson's expenditures were not motivated by financial return. He could have lost every penny and been financially sound and, one believes, spiritually fulfilled as well. The creation of films that simply should exist, and using Christian funds to do it, is a sound use of money. The justification is the film, not a financial return.

Are other Christian investors with billions to invest ready to join in a world-changing venture? Another favorite film of mine is *The Mission*. It tells the story of Jesuits from Spain leaving all worldly safety behind and coming to the new world to change it as an act of Christian faith. In the shadow of some of the four-hundred-year-old missions they built in a region called Alta California, a radical new opportunity of faith exists to change the world for the better, again.

Originally from Portsmouth, Rhode Island, **Barbara Nicolosi** has an M.A. in Television and Film from Northwestern University, Evanston, Illinois, and a B.A. from the Great Books Program at Magdalen College in Warner, New Hampshire. She is adjunct professor of screenwriting at Azusa Pacific University in Azusa, California.

Ms. Nicolosi is the executive director of Act One, Inc., a nonprofit training and formation program for Hollywood writers and executives. Act One keynotes artistry, professionalism, ethics, and Christian spirituality. A screenwriter herself, Ms. Nicolosi has several projects in development.

Ms. Nicolosi has been a panelist for the National Endowment for the Arts and a reader for the Humanitas prize. She is the author of a monthly column on media in the *National Catholic Register* and was the recipient of Catholic Press Awards in 2000 and 2002. Her popular blog, "Church of the Masses" (www.churchofthemasses.blogspot.com), receives thousands of visitors every week.

**Spencer Lewerenz** is the associate director of the Act One: Writing for Hollywood Program. He has a B.A. in English from the University of Dallas and graduate studies in English at the University of Texas at Dallas. He attended the National Journalism Center in Washington, D.C. He worked on the editorial staff of the *Washington Times* and the America's Future Foundation, both in Washington, D.C. He was the culture editor for *The World and I* magazine. Along with numerous editorials for the *Washington Times*, Mr. Lewerenz has written ten articles for the magazines *First Things*, *Doublethink*, and *Crisis*.